WEST YORKS WALKS

CALDERDALE & BRADFORD

Martin Brewis

Published by Sigma Leisure – an imprint of
Sigma Press, 1 South Oak Lane, Wilmslow, Cheshire SK9 6AR, England.

British Library Cataloguing in Publication Data
A CIP record for this book is available from the British Library.

ISBN: 1-85058-722-1

Cover Design: MFP Design and Print

Typesetting and Design by: Sigma Press, Wilmslow, Cheshire.

Cover photographs: Shibden Hall; stone staircase in Luddenden Dean; Cow and Calf Crags, Ilkley.

Maps: the author

Photographs: John Holmes

Printed by: MFP Design and Print

Disclaimer: the information in this book is given in good faith and is believed to be correct at the time of publication. No responsibility is accepted by either the author or publisher for errors or omissions, or for any loss or injury howsoever caused. Only you can judge your own fitness, competence and experience.

Preface

Walks should be good exercise and good fun. They would seem to be pointless unless they contained both these elements. In every walk I have tried to combine both elements, and furthermore, find something that will be of interest to all members of the family, of whatever age.

There should also be an element of the unpredictable and of mystery. Whereas the descriptions and maps are very detailed, almost to the point of defying the walker to get lost, there will always be something that is not totally clear, and where the walker has to make a calculated decision. Indeed, the walks are only accurate on the day that they were checked. It never ceases to amaze me how much changes and in particular with the different seasons. What is an easy path in one season can be ploughed up, overgrown or underwater in another; splendid views of landmarks at one time can be obliterated by trees in full foliage or by overcast weather at another.

Now for the mystery element: in my former professional existence, I tried to inculcate into young minds the spirit of enquiry. So, I have framed a question in every walk about some 'mystery'. Frankly, I do not know the answers to some questions, so, please, I ask you to e-mail your suggestions to me at: wywalks@yahoo.co.uk

Acknowledgements

This book would not exist but for the time and effort of others. I am much indebted to the following: John Holmes, who has walked - at mapping pace - with unfailing good humour, and photographed points of interest on every route; my army of 'checkers', who, bless them, have become hooked on their 'task', including retired secondary head colleagues, Bob Etherington, Brian Evans, Allan Newton, David Rogerson, Cliff Simpkin and Clive Watkins, as well as friends of the chief adviser, Geoff Wilson, Arthur and Audrey Darkin, Brian Hopper and Stanley Ashton - without whose acute observational skills and advice the directions and maps would be less than accurate; and especially to my wife, who has long suffered my not being around, engrossed as I have been with walking, mapping and computerising the routes.

Points of Interest

1: Addingham: Why is Addingham so historic?
2: Ilkley Moor: What was the purpose of these stones?
3: Ilkley Riverside: Opposite Calvary, what is the purpose of the stone steps?
4: Silsden: What is the local name for this 'Dale'? What is the origin of the Tower?

5: Bingley: What was the original product of Holroyd Mill?
6: Mortons: Why the spelling of Busfeild?
7: Eldwick: Where did the Monksway go from and to?
8: Cullingworth: Where did the railway start and finish?
9: Harden: Where does the quotation come from?
10: Haworth: What date is MDCCLII?
11: Oxenhope: What are the meanings of 'Yate' and 'Farra'?
12: Tong: Who were/are the Moravians?

13: Gauxholme: What is the origin of the names: Gauxholme, Naze, Gorpley and Pexwood?
14: Mankinholes: Why was 'London Road' so called?
15: Todmorden: Who is Hudson's Bridge named after?
16: Cragg Vale: What do you notice about the way the stones were laid at Higher Cragg?
17: Stoodley Pike: What used to happen at this pillar in olden times?
18: Hebden Dale: (A+B) Why was the wall so built? (C) What sort of tree are they holding?
19: Luddenden Dean: Where is the well?
20: Rishworth: Why was the wall so solidly built?

21: Calder + Hebble: Why Fall Ing and where is it?
22: Greetland: What is the 'water feature'? What is the meaning of the two phrases 'Honest Water' and 'Pro Bono Publico'? What was the original purpose of the Wainhouse Tower?
23: Ogden: Why might this Gap be aptly named?
24: Norcliffe: What is historically wrong on the plaque at the bottom of Holloway?
25: Norwood Green: What is the local name of this woodland?
26: Shibden: Why such a remarkable feature?

If you wish to be interactive, e-mail suggestions to: wywalks@yahoo.co.uk

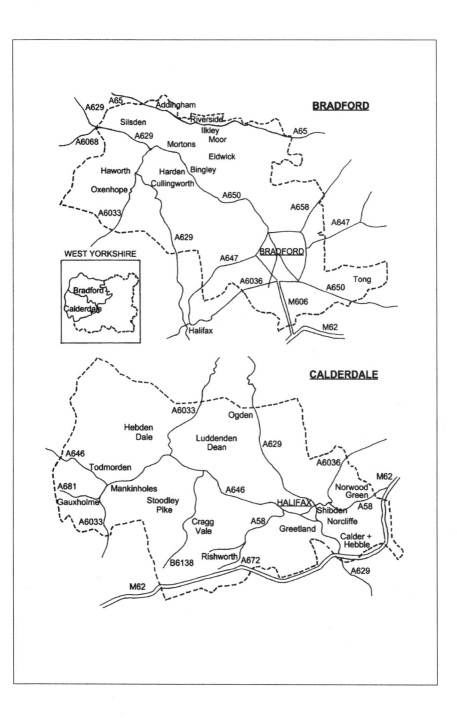

Contents

Introduction

The Walks

KEY to MAPS

		Stiles:		
∞∞∞	Wall		fence	⊟
┼┼┼┼┼	Fence		stone/wall	⊟
≋	Hedge		fence + wall	⊟
⌐	Metalled road/lane		metal	⊟
– – –	Walker's track		metal bar	⊟
– – –	Track		zigzag	⊞
∿	Stream		pillar	⊔
∿	Water		ladder	⊟
⌣	Bridge		V-shaped	∀
ꝰ⋏ꝰ	Trees		wall gap	∪
⧻	Steps	Gates:	fence	⊠
⊟	Cattle grid		metal	Ⅲ
╫	Railway		farm type	⊠
⥄	Gateposts		kissing	∈

Calderdale and Bradford

The districts of Calderdale and Bradford comprise the western part of West Yorkshire, dominated by the main and tributary valleys of two rivers, Calder and Aire, and their associated canals. Halifax, the best preserved of all Calderdale towns, set in a narrow cleft, had until the industrial revolution a dour reputation "From Hull, Hell and Halifax, good Lord, deliver us!" Bradford, with its buildings of Pennine stone, was the old world capital of wool.

Whilst in the past these areas have been associated with a predominantly industrial landscape, you may well be surprised to find vast areas of rolling Pennine moorland intersected by steep-sided secluded wooded valleys, deans and cloughs. Scattered here and there are rugged stone villages and outlying hill farms connected by fascinating packhorse trails, known locally as 'causeys'. The whole Brontë-type landscape seems held together by criss-crossing dry stone walls which give the area its rugged gritstone character.

About this Book

The 26 walks fall into four geographical areas (see location maps):

North Bradford: the countryside between the valleys of the Rivers Wharfe and (Upper) Aire, south of A65 and north of A650/629, taking in the towns of Addingham, Silsden and Ilkley. (Walks 1 to 4)

South Bradford: to the north of Bingley, the countryside south of A650 and on either side of the Worth Valley and A629 from Halifax to Keighley, and eccentrically, a trio of walks around Tong, east of Bradford. (Walks 5 to 12)

West Calderdale: the area covered by the Calder and tributary valleys, from the East Lancs border in the west to Halifax in the east. (Walks 13 to 20)

East Calderdale: countryside to the east of Halifax, south of Bradford, and bordered by Kirklees to the south and east. (Walks 21 to 26)

Distances

The walks vary in length from 5 to 14 kilometres (3 to 9 miles). All distances are inevitably approximate and a guide only. I have used kilometres and metres (with a conversion to miles in brackets) – the walker covers kilometres more quickly!

Times

The time to complete a walk varies for all sorts of reasons. Every walker has her/his own comfortable pace; the terrain varies from level to undulating ground or to steep inclines and descents; weather conditions or seasons of the year change the state of paths; and, you may wish to linger at points of interest. I have therefore assumed that the average walker will complete an uninterrupted walk at 3 kilometres (2 miles) per hour. Depending on the distance, the routes will entail a brisk morning or afternoon walk; some can easily be a full day's ramble, including a picnic or refreshment stop on the way.

Maps and Descriptions

I have quoted from the Ordnance Survey Landranger Series (1:50 000) and where applicable the Outdoor Leisure and/or Explorer Series (1:25 000), with a grid reference for the starting point of the walk. The maps and descriptions are intentionally very detailed in an attempt to keep you always on the right track. Indeed, each type of stile and gate is detailed so that you can recognise exactly where you are. I have used the shorthand (L) and (R) to avoid the constant repetition of the longer phrases 'on your left/right'. To pinpoint your position on the walks, numbers at the beginning of paragraphs in the route descriptions relate to numbered points on the maps.

All the walks have been rewalked and checked independently of the author, but accuracy in every detail is impossible, as features change with surprising rapidity.

Terrain

I have indicated, but not graded, the sort of terrain over which you will be walking, and especially if there are steep stretches up or downhill. Generally, the routes follow the easier contours. I have kept the amount of roadwalking to a minimum, assuming that walkers prefer countryside paths. To the best of my knowledge, in consultation with the Countryside Service Officers in Bradford (Jayne Benson) and Calderdale (Ian Kendall), all the routes are rights of way or permissive paths.

The state of the terrain varies enormously according to the season and the current weather. You will find on all walks wet, muddy or boggy patches, and therefore, I would advise that you wear walking boots or tough waterproof shoes in all seasons. You may think that shorts are suitable for summer walking, but beware nettles and brambles. Again, I would advise always taking a waterproof jacket and trousers, and other walking 'equipment' should include a compass, whistle, extra pullover, food and liquid.

Parking and Refreshments

Most of the walks are accessible by bus, but I have not given details as routes, numbers and timetables can change unpredictably. The telephone number for Metro Services is: 0113 245 7676. There are also good train services out of Manchester, Leeds and Bradford (Tel. No: 0345 48 49 50).

I have indicated possible parking 'in the vicinity of'. If in doubt, please ask permission on the spot to avoid any offence or displeasure. Possible places to obtain refreshment have been listed on or nearby the walks, and there will be others.

Points of Interest

Whilst this is a book of walks, and neither a historical nor geographical guide, the 'points of interest' are what really make a walk enjoyable. The walk directions and the points of interest are clearly separated and displayed in contrasting fonts. I have also put a summary description of the walk before the start of the directions.

Whilst the countryside is there for us all to enjoy, remember that for farmers and others the countryside is their business and livelihood, and so we all depend on mutual goodwill. That said, enjoy the exercise, fun and mystery of walking in Calderdale and Bradford.

1: Addingham

Moorside Upland Views

Distance: 5.8 km (3⅔ miles) or 5 km (3 miles) with shortcut

Time: 2 hours

Map: OS Outdoor Leisure 21 (1:25 000), Landranger 104 (1:50 000)

Parking: on the main street of Addingham, in the vicinity of the Craven Heifer (an 1820 building on the site of a 1687 public house), grid reference: 072498

Terrain: meadow, field and woodland, farm track and path, and only one short stretch of road – most of the first section of the walk is uphill with moderately steep ascents, and gentle descents on the return section

Refreshments: available in Addingham at the Craven Heifer, the Sailor and other public houses

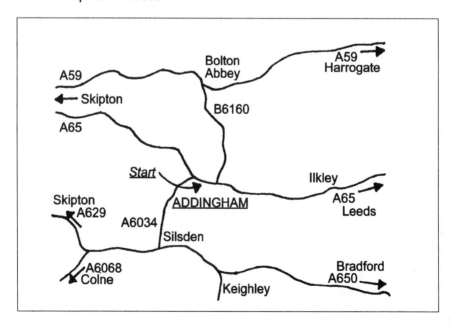

Gildersber

THIS most pleasant, if slightly strenuous, walk starts and finishes in the village of Addingham, which has a number of historic buildings of interest. You start by going up a delightful hidden valley, and after crossing the by-pass you ascend via a succession of farms to gain extensive views over to Ilkley Moor and a brief glimpse of Bolton Abbey across the valley. A special feature of the walk is the numerous small wooden gates. Why is Addingham so historic?

Starting with the Craven Heifer at your back, walk down the road for 100 metres. Turn acutely right up behind a row of workshops of Townhead Trading Centre. At the top of the car park go through a small wooden gate and up beside Marchup Beck (R). Veer left up a steep bit to two small wooden gates over wall stiles on either side of a road. Bear right down to and walk up past a fence and the stream (R). Go on and over a wall stile into a wood. Bear left through a wood fence gate, up left and over a wooden bridge. Halfway up a steep bank, go through a fence gate (R). Going up left follow the fence (L) to the top left-hand corner, cross left over the beck and up to a wooden kissing gate. Climb the wooden steps and cross the by-pass road (A65).

1.   Straight ahead go through the wooden kissing gate, turn right and then left up and alongside Dark Wood (R). Depending on the state of the field crops, follow the wall to the top right-hand corner, then left across to double wooden gates (or, veer diagonally left over the field to the gates). Go over the track, through other double gates and walk up the field diagonally left to a farm gate at the top. Go straight ahead, and over the junction of farm tracks on a broad track towards a farm. Go past a pole (R) and through a metal gate or over a fence/wall stile (R). Go round to the right passing in front of farm buildings (R), possibly through a series of metal gates. Continue a short distance, and turn left onto a lane and through a metal gate by Gildersber Farm. Turn right with the lane down to the road (Cocking Lane).

2.   Crossing the road go straight on through a farm gate and up towards High Brockabank. Once you cross a cattle grid, you have a choice of routes:

3(a) If you want to keep at this level, go straight on to Brockabank Farm (1546): just before the farm take the permissive path, bearing left over a wall stile, right for 10 metres to a wall stile, and down past the wall (R) to a wall stile (R). Go ahead and turn left in the angle of walls. Continue over the field to a wall stile by an elm tree (L), onto a track between a wall (L) and fence (R). Walk on past a stone pillar with slots, keeping beside the fence to a wooden gate (R) – and go straight on (see 6 below);

If you choose to climb up high to get the views, look back to glimpse Chelker Reservoir and Bolton Abbey nestling in the valley:

3(b) Alternatively, after the cattle grid turn right up by a fence (L) to a wall stile. Carry on up alongside a plantation (L) to a fence stile at the top. Carry on to go over a fence stile with a stone gatepost with three well-defined slot holes. Go alongside a wall (L) to a wall stile, followed by another, and bear right round a barn to a wall stile. Opposite is a stone water trough.

4.   Turn left through a wooden farm gate down between the farm buildings (High House). Turn right round its bottom end and, after viewing the fine front façade of the house, bend left over a fence down a sunken path. You come to a beck; cross it by way of the stones and go left through a metal gate. Keep going down close by the line of the trees and gully (L). At the bottom go through a wooden farm gate beside an overgrown and deserted farm.

This farmhouse was 'Cuckoo Nest', once the home of the brothers

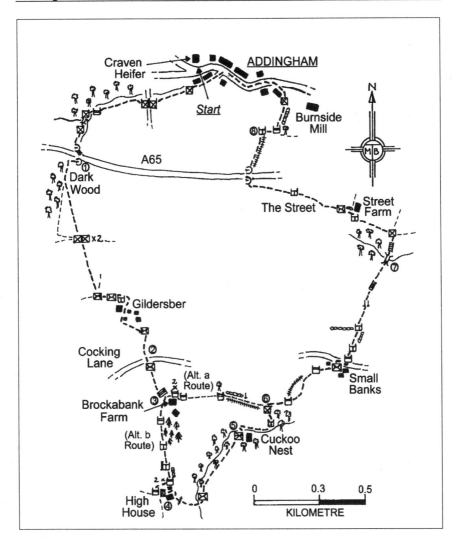

Fido, who, according to Thelma Thompson of Brockabank Farm, used to entertain children by feeding mice, kept in dresser drawers!

5. Turn left, cross the stream and follow it (R) downhill. At the bottom in the left-hand corner against the wood, cross a fence + wall stile over a wall. Cross the field to a wooden gate + wall stile and turn right.

As you walk along, briefly glimpse Bolton Abbey (L) and look across to Ilkley Moor (R). At Small Banks ahead view the house opposite from the right-hand side, with SHS 1785 over its front door, and the barn (L) dated SRS 1772.

6. Go along the track to a wall stile. As you bear left round the edge of the field, you come to a wall stile beside a wall (L) and farm gate (R). Go down the track and through a wooden gate. Now at Small Banks, zigzag left and right past a barn (L). Go onto the road for 40 metres and left over a wall stile, then a fence stile (+ dog stile) and down the field beside a wall (R) to a fence stile. Go straight over the field to a stone pillar stile, down stone steps and alongside a wall/fence (R) to a bridge over a stream.

7. Go down into and out of a dip up stone steps to a small wooden gate. Turn left to a fence + wall stile between an old oak tree (L) and wall (R). Walk past Street Farm (R) with its buttressed wall and on up a lane through a metal gate. As the track bends right to a metal gate, go straight on to a fence stile and between trees. As the path nears the road, in the hedge (R) is a wooden kissing gate. Cross A65 to a similar gate and go straight down alongside a fence (R).

8. At the bottom of the field turn right over a fence stile. Going on between overgrown walls, just before an oak tree and a fence, cross a wall stile (L). Go down the field to a small wooden gate. Over the wall (R) is Burnside Mill. Passing Beckfoot and Well House Cottages (L), bear left up by the beck (R). You emerge opposite High Bank and pass The Sailor (L). Carry on up the main street passing a lane (R) to Cockshotts Place. Return to wherever you have parked your car.

Historical points of interest:

Burnside Mill: a steam driven silk spinning mill (1870).

High Bank: inscribed CIM 1790, home of the Cunliffes, owners of Low Mill.

The Sailor: originally a 17th century thatched cottage.

Cockshotts Place: a working loom shop (1812).

2: Ilkley Moor

Standing Stones

Distance: 8.8 km (5½ miles)

Time: 3 hours

Map: OS Landranger 104 (1:50 000)

Parking: off the Ilkley Moor road, at the Cow and Calf car park, grid reference: 133467

Terrain: open moorland paths

Refreshments: at a refreshments hut (not always open) at the Cow and Calf car park, or down in Ilkley

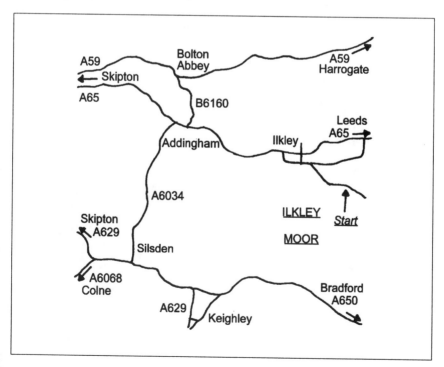

THIS is not just a walk: it does initially take you up steepish paths
past quarry workings and crags, and thereafter on open moorland
paths; but the moor also has several sites of interest which may well
surprise you!

Starting from the car park, with your back to Ilkley, head up the path
straight for the Cow and Calf crags. As you near them, walk up the
left-hand side of them and bear round right to head off over open country in a south-westerly direction towards Ilkley Crags on the horizon.
You cross a stream and rise up to the top, where you continue in the
same direction. When you reach the large cairn at the next cross-paths,
turn left onto the Dales Way.

1. You eventually reach Gill Head; cross the stream and go up stone steps
    and continue, including a stretch over duckboarding. At the next rise
    there is a standing stone (R) with inscriptions: TP on one end; IM ILB
    1893 on one face, and on the backside WM with an indistinct date –
    1835? 150 metres further on (L) there is an imposing stone circle called
    'The Twelve Apostles'. Carry on to the next cross-paths where there is a
    stone with (on different faces) mile distances in Roman numerals: To
    Eldwick, Saltaire and Bingley V; Ilkley II (and 2 miles carved in a differ-
    ent hand), with a mason's mark be-
    low.

2. Immediately at the fork in the path
    bear left on the lesser path through
    the heather past small metal posts.
    Eventually crossing a wall stile,
    bear gently round left and past a
    large boulder (L). You come on your
    left to two wall stiles.

    One stile has metal bars and the
    other has its right-hand post
    carved: Thos pullcyn Horncliffe
    Well, and below it a boundary
    stone carved with GLF. Take time
    to detour over this stile to view a
    small standing stone with the
    inscription, W+M Horncliffe Well,
    and the foundation remains of
    substantial buildings beyond.

Inscribed standing stone

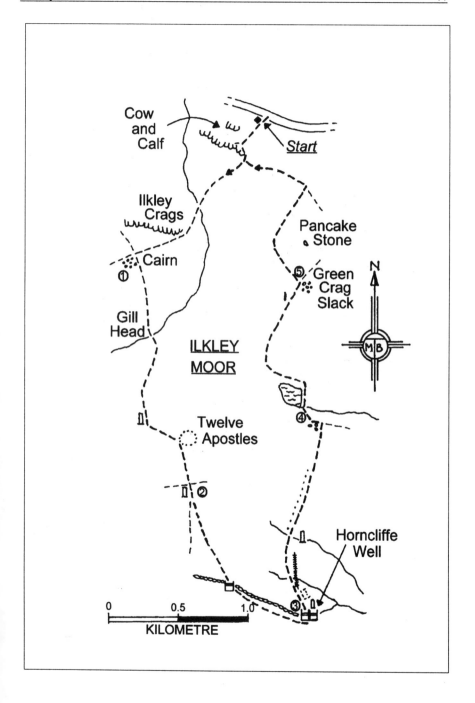

From hereon, if walking in the second half of August, beware of grouse shooting!

3. Return to cross the left-hand stile and head back across the moor in a northerly direction, initially beside a wire fence (R). After a beck there is another standing stone away to your right: "Thos pullcyn" on one side, and on the rear "Walter Hawksworth" – what was the purpose of these stones? Along this stretch, you pass on your left a row of ten stone circle enclosures constructed for grouse shooting. At rocks on the crest of the ridge turn left, and shortly fork off to the right.

4. Walk down and over the wall and stepping stones to go along the dam wall of the reservoir, which in wetter times was much larger. Bend round left and then right up and over the crest of the rise with a yellow pole (L). At the next outcrop, Green Crag Slack, view the various carvings: W+M 1785, ILB 1893, and TP on the backside.

5. Bear left and walk downhill until you bear round right down a gully path. Continue down to a junction of paths. Turn left and go up over the rise. Bear right down past the Cow and Calf (L) and return to your car.

As you descend from the gully, look right to view the Pancake Stone, the overhanging rock balancing on others, and take in the fine view over Ilkley.

3: Ilkley

Riverside Views

Distance: 8 km (5 miles)

Time: 2½ hours

Map: OS Landranger 104 (1:50 000)

Parking: west of the A65 crossroads in Ilkley, take one of the roads right off A65 and park anywhere on Riverside Gardens, grid reference: 115478

Terrain: meadow, field and woodland, farm track, path and short stretches of road – mainly on the level with a couple of moderate ascents and one descent through woodland

Refreshments: available in Ilkley

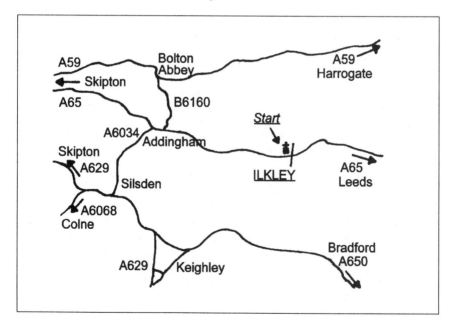

THIS is a most pleasant walk starting and finishing alongside the River Wharfe very close to the centre of Ilkley. After a stretch of woodland and open country you track up onto a ridge above Ilkley, affording extensive views. You return by descending through woodland and over a suspension bridge. You can finish by looking round the Parish Church and Manor House.

The first bridge is known locally as the 'Roman Bridge'. On its parapet (R) you can see the flood levels: Nov 23, 1866, and Dec 14 1936.

Start by walking in a westerly direction alongside the River Wharfe. You soon come to the 'Roman Bridge' with its flood levels recorded (R). Climb the stone steps and turn right over the bridge. At the opposite end you can see a gas-type lamp (R) on a wooden stand. Turn left through wooden gates and wind your way along the bank. Bend left alongside the golf course (L). Where the path meets the road, turn uphill and almost immediately turn left into and up Owler Park Road.

1. At the top of the road, on your left is a wall stile with a metal bar. Walk into a wood (signposted to Nesfield). Wind your way through the wood and cross a fence stile, with dog stile, out of it. Go across the field bearing slightly left to cross stepping stones. Then bear right between a fence (L) and trees (R) to cross a beck and a fence stile.

2. Go up a short steep incline and round right to a fence stile. Go down wooden steps and over a wooden bridge. Bear left and keep right of the boundary fence of Low Austby passing a magnificent oak (L). Cross a fence stile and continue alongside a fir plantation (R) between widely spaced fences. Follow the wall (L) round to a wall stile in the corner. Go across the field aiming for the windmill on the horizon to a fence stile. Do NOT cross – just pause here.

On the knoll in the field ahead, left of Scarr House (Nesfield), is the outline of a former fort, Castleberg.

3. Turn acutely round right, and with the metal gate at your back, walk ahead on a track leading uphill, keeping left of hawthorn trees. You come to a wall stile with a sheephole (L). Cross it and follow a wall (L) all the way up and alongside a wood (L) over slabs to a small wooden gate in a wall stile. Walk on in front of High Austby (L) and bear up left past several topiary-type holly bushes. Passing a laurel hedge (L) go to a wall stile.

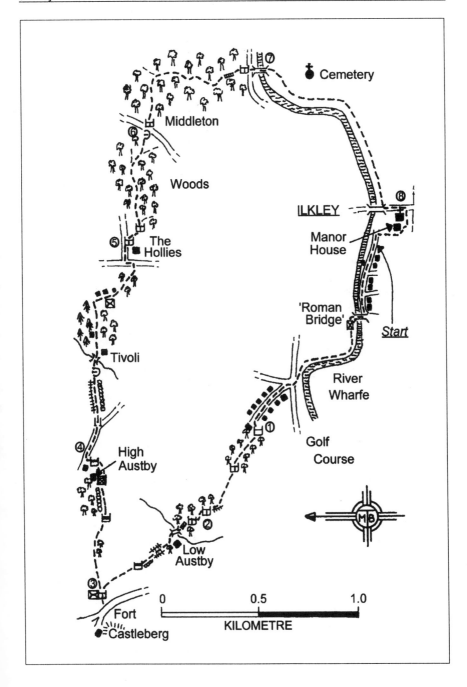

Cemetery

Middleton

Woods

⑦

⑥

ILKLEY

⑧

Manor
House

The
Hollies

⑤

'Roman
Bridge'

Start

Tivoli

River
Wharfe

④

High
Austby

Golf
Course

①

②

Low
Austby

③

Fort
Castleberg

0   0.5   1.0

KILOMETRE

As you go up the lane, the house (L) has a fine stepped chimney, and on the lane side is 'Margaret's Garden', planted around a tree.

4. At the junction turn right. In 220 metres go straight on through wooden gateposts with a metal post in the middle. Going between a fence (L) and wall (R), at the other end you can go through a wooden kissing (or metal) gate. Go over a beck, also bridged (L), and past Tivoli (R) up the lane through an avenue of trees. Opposite Calvary are stone steps—for what purpose? Continue through a wood of fir (L) and deciduous trees (R), bending right with the lane. At the junction, with metal gates (R) and The Mistral (L), veer left. Go down beside a fence (L) on a track through trees. Bear left onto a lane. At a T-junction turn left for 40 metres, then right towards Middleton Hospital past The Hollies (R).

From here onwards, you get a fine view over Ilkley to the Crags and the Cow and Calf Hotel.

5. On past a metal gate, cross a fence stile (R) and bear diagonally left down across the field, passing a large lone tree (R). Cross a fence stile into the wood. At the bottom of the first slope, before the right bend, cross the beck ahead. Continue straight on a undulating but generally downhill path through the wood. You pass a seat (L). At the forks take the right and left ones on the main path down to a wooden kissing gate.

6. Cross the road and go over a fence stile into the wood. Bear left keeping the wall (R) and go over some boggy parts. At the end of the wall turn right downhill. (There are lots of paths hereabouts, and provided you keep doing downhill you will eventually come out onto a road). As the path levels out bear right. Cross stepping stones. Go up, over rise and down and round left between silver birches. Eventually go gently round right to a fence stile. Cross the road and go straight over the (1934) suspension bridge across the River Wharfe.

7. Turn right onto a path and walk eventually between metal and wood fences, and past a cemetery on your left. Continue on this path until you come to the road bridge. It is suggested that you take time to make a diversion here. Go right up the steps, turn left and walk up to and enter the church.

Inside, at the west end are two altars, dating from the period of the Roman garrison, which have been reshaped and possibly used as heads of windows, deflecting the light downwards; also there are three Saxon crosses, dating from late 8th- early 9th century.

Outside, and on the west end of the Manor House, there is a plaque – 'Roman Fort, Olicana, AD 79, West Gate'.

8. Exiting from the church, turn right and go down the steps to view the magnificent front of the Manor House. Turn right round its west end, through a small wooden gate and go down the slope to turn left onto the riverside path and to your car.

Riverside, Ilkley

4: Silsden

Becks and Woodlands Galore

Distance: 8 km (5 miles)

Time: 2½ hours

Map: OS Outdoor Leisure 21 (1:25 000), Landranger 104 (1:50 000)

Parking: in Brown Bank Lane or North Street at Town Head, grid reference: 046469

Terrain: meadow, field and woodland, farm track, path and short stretches of road – the walk is undulating with the only steepish ascent soon after the start

Refreshments: the nearest are at the Kings'Arms and the Punch Bowl, but there are plenty down in Silsden, as well as at Meadmore's Restaurant, after 2.5 km

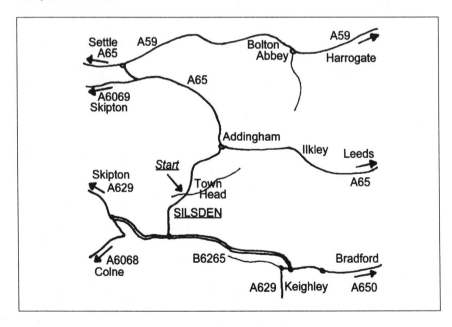

THIS walk is a most pleasant and varied stroll, starting and finishing at the top (north) end of Silsden. It takes you through some gorgeous scenery, woodlands and over hidden becks – what is the local name for this 'Dale'? – before affording you wide views down over Airedale as you return through the delightful hamlets of Swartha and Brunthwaite. A special feature of this walk is the number of stepped stone stiles.

Starting at Town Head walk westwards along North Street past Town Head Farm (R). Turn right into Breakmoor Avenue and immediately left at a right (not acute) angle. Go straight on to a grassy track between bungalows to a fence stile with stone steps. Bear diagonally right downhill keeping right of a large tree to cross a metal bridge with handrails. Follow the fence (L) round to an elongated fence stile and on to a stone pillar stile. This is the first woodland and beck, Hayhills Beck. Veer left under two sets of power lines to the top left side of the wood.

1. At the top of the field, go over a fence stile with a metal gate (L). Go on between a wall (L) and fence (R). At the wall ahead go over a wall stile and the follow the hedge (L). At the top end of the field, 15 metres short of farm buildings, cross a stream (L) and a fence stile. Turn right following the hedge and fence to a wall stile in the right-hand corner. Go over the ditch and turn right onto the track to Hay Hills Farm. Cross the wall stile with 'The Lermans' (R). Veer slightly left over the tarmac lane, then go over the stone slab bridge and wall stile. Walk diagonally left over the field to a fence stile. Continue up the field beside the gully and beck (R).

Stepped stile

2.   At a fence stile go right down a tunnel of bushes to cross a beck over a
     stone slab bridge and up stone steps to a fence stile – a delightful spot.
     Go alongside the gully (L) and round left to a wall stile with steps. Pass
     Ivy House (R) and go straight on up the tarmac drive and on through the
     open gateway up a dirt track. At a garage with metal door ahead, turn
     right in front of cottages (L) to a stepped wall stile. Go left through a
     small wooden gate into a field. Shortly, cross a fence stile and go up be-
     tween a wall (L) and fence (R) to a wall stile. Follow a higher wall (R) to a
     stepped wall stile. Go straight on passing Dales Bank Farm (R).
     [Meadmore's Restaurant – for a drink and sandwiches is down to the
     right].

3.   Veer slightly right to a fence stile. Keep on alongside the hedge and
     over a fence stile. Go over a track and wall stile with guard rail, then
     straight over the field to a wall stile on the far side. Carry on over the
     track and alongside a willow hedge (L) to a fence stile in the corner.
     Take the stone steps down to a wooden bridge over Foster Cliff Beck –
     another picturesque scene. Go up and over the tarmac drive to a small
     metal gate. Turn right at the wall ((R) and go to another small metal
     gate. Follow the wall (R) for some 100 metres to turn right through a
     third gate. Follow the line of the fence (R).

     You can see an old tower standing proud over the horizon (L) – what
     is its origin?

4.   At the bottom go between gorse (L) and hawthorn (R) down wooden
     steps on a zigzag path and over the wall stile. Turn left alongside the
     beck, following it round right until you cross it as it flows into the main
     stream. Go on to turn left, crossing Great Gill Beck on a metal bridge
     with handrails and go up the stone steps – this is the fourth delightful
     piece of woodland on this walk. Follow the track round right and veer left
     up between hawthorn trees.

5.   At some scattered rocks, turn left at right angles and go up the slope
     passing a large rock (R). You emerge onto open land. Follow the fence
     (L) up the field to a stepped wall stile topped by pillars. Crossing a track,
     ignore a high ladder stile (L) and carry on beside the wall (L) to a
     stepped wall stile. Go alongside a fence, then wall (L) to a wall stile with
     metal bars. Continue to a wall gap with a small wooden gate on the left
     of a metal farm gate. You gain a good view of Silsden Reservoir (R).
     Turn left up a concrete drive past Lower Cringles Farm with a shepherd
     and dog weather vane (R) to a high wall stile with wooden gate. Go
     straight over past a barn (L) to a wall stile with wooden gate. Turn right
     down the main road for 240 metres.

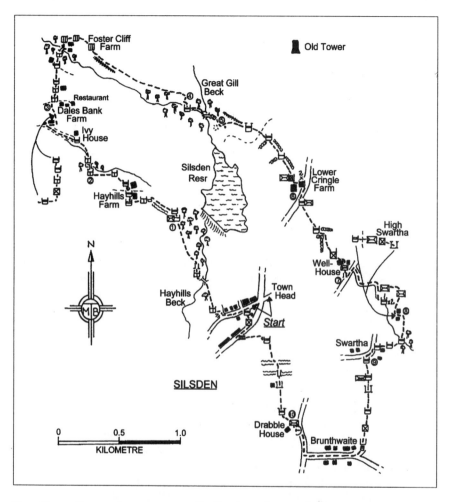

6. Cross the road, go over a wall stile, then diagonally right across the field to a wall stile in the corner. Turn left up between walls, then right alongside the wall (R), but heading for the farmhouse ahead. Go through a small wooden gate to the right of a telegraph pole. Bear left of the stone garage and round to the metal gate. There is a large dovecote on a pole (R). Go straight on the tarmac drive to go through stone gateposts at the end.

7. Turn left up Brown Bank Lane for 40 metres. Turn right into Swartha Lane and past a wooden seat (L). After zigzag bends, you come to a wall stile (L). Note: having crossed the wall, it may be very overgrown —

it may be difficult to go down to a bridge, cross the stream, and then up to the right and over a wall stile! If difficult, you may care to backtrack a few metres to the last bend and turn right on the track down to a wooden farm gate. From this, bear right to a wooden farm gate in mid-wall. Turn right through it and head straight for the bottom side of the barn, and left up its far side to the wall stile (see Inset on map).

8. Go over a farm track and up between buildings to a metal gate. Veer right to a wooden farm gate, a pillar wall stile and alongside a wall (R) to a pillar wall stile with stone steps on its far side. Bear right downhill to the corner of a wood and a wall stile. Go over a brook to the top of the rise. Cross the stepped wall stile (R). Turn left alongside the wall (L) to a wall stile and down stone steps into the lane. Turn left past Swartha House Farm.

From hereon there is a fine view over the Airedale Valley.

9. On the right bend, cross the wall stile (L) down over the field to a wall stile. Go on down the field to a very narrow slab pillar stile with, in front of it, a stone gatepost with three square postholes. Carry on down to another wall stile, then a small wooden gate and a wall gap with stone steps. Bend right into the village of Brunthwaite in front of houses (R). A house garage (L) has a 'leaping' fish weather vane. You pass Otter Croft (L) with its otter door window. Turn right at the T-junction and walk on to bear left at Drabble House through a metal kissing gate. Go on through a metal gate right of the farm.

10. Cross the field diagonally to a wall stile with pillar slabs. Keep alongside the wall (R) to a wood and stone pillar stile to the right of a barn. Veer left over the field to a squeeze stone pillar stile in a hedge, then across to a gap in the hedge. Cross the field to a wall stile in the far-left corner and over into an allotment. Go right round the angles and down stone steps onto the road. Cross the road and turn right. Just past a bus stop, go through a small wooden gate (L), a wall (R) to a wall stile, and to wherever you have parked your car.

5: Bingley

Five-Rise Locks and a Manor House

Distance: 7.2 km (4½ miles) or, with Walk 6: 14.4 km (9 miles)

Time: 2½ hours or, with Walk 6, 4½ hours

Map: OS Explorer 288 (1:25 000), Landranger 104 (1:50 000)

Parking: in the car park on the north side of Bingley Station, off A650 (pay and display), grid reference: 108392

Terrain: along the canal bank at the start and finish, path, track and short stretches of road, and one steepish ascent

Refreshments: several in Bingley

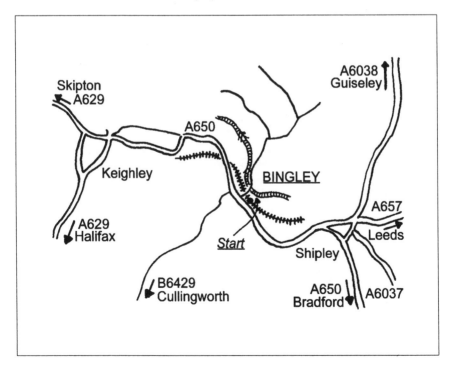

THIS pleasant walk is easy at the start and finish along the bank of the Leeds and Liverpool canal. It takes you past the famous Three-and Five-Rise Locks. Leaving the canal, you go up through a wooded glen to the charming hamlet of Micklethwaite, where there is a former Manor House. Micklethwaite, (Muceltoit meaning 'Great Clearing') was a 10th century Viking settlement. Thereafter, you have a steep walk up above Bingley – the reward is a gentle descent down a secluded and wooded valley before returning beside the canal.

Starting with the station (L), walk in a north westerly direction and up steps onto the roadway. Turn right and cross the canal bridge. Turn left down the ramp onto the canal side, signposted 'Waterbus'. In 300 metres you reach Three-Rise Locks. Cross the canal to the left bank and continue for 500 metres to the Five-Rise Locks.

The Locks are an impressive sight, rising over 59 feet in a distance of 320 feet. The canal was built in 1774, the distance to Leeds being 16 miles and to Liverpool 111 miles.

1.   Continue on the canal side going through metal gates before the next bridge. Go on past Micklethwaite Wharf and further on you go through another set of metal gates and to Lingcroft Wharf. Turn right over the swing bridge, noting the old pump by the gate (R) as well as the weather vane of a blacksmith and anvil on the shed roof.

2.   Going past the driveway (R) and mirror, in 10 metres turn right through a wall gap and down stone steps, and on between fences. 100 metres up and alongside a big tree (R), turn right over a fence and beside a wall (L) down to a stone crossing of a stream. Veer up left and over and under fallen trees to a fence stile. Go left along the field keeping on the path down close to the stream (L), as it cascades down. Continue to a fence stile, then go on between fences to a fence plus wall stile. On your right is the converted Holroyd Mill – what was the original product of the mill? Go on beside the stream, round right up wooden and stone steps, then left up beside a metal railing. Cross the mill pond overflow on wooden beams. Go straight on, ignoring a little bridge (R), and over a stone slab bridge. Turn right on a wooden bridge over the inflow channel, and go up the bank alongside several mini-weirs to a wall stile.

3.   [NB. You can join this walk up with 'The Mortons' Walk 6. Turn left and cross a metal bridge with railings, and go up a narrowing path. At the top turn left into Cliffe Mill Fold and go rightish up Dimples Lane, turning left onto the main road to the Memorial Institute (L). See Walk 6.]

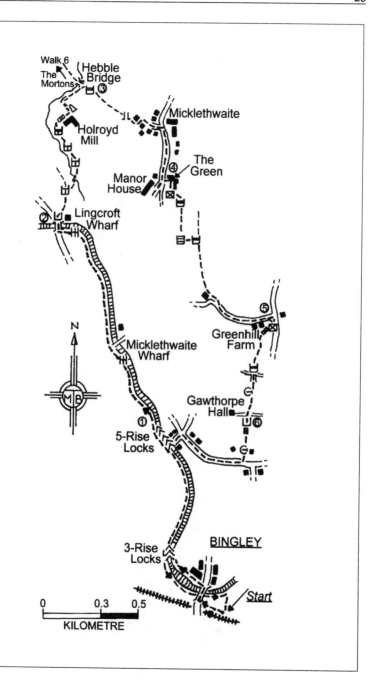

If continuing on Walk 5, turn right up the track between initially narrow, then wider spaced walls. Go on through stone gateposts and onto a tarmac lane. Turn left up past Beck Farm Barn (R) to bend right past Beck House (R), with its horse and foal weather vane. Veer left up past the Methodist Free Church (R) in Beck Road. At the top turn right into and down High Fold (Micklethwaite). Go past the bungalows to The Green (L).

Take the time to walk a few metres further on to turn right into Victoria Street and see the Manor House AD 1601. Butler's Fold, later on the walk, is named after a former local landowner, and his daughter's name is remembered in Bessie Lane.

The Manor House, Micklethwaite

4. Retrace your steps and turn right up The Green. At the top turn right and walk down onto a cobbled lane past Woodlands Barn (L) and Butler's Fold cottages beyond. Go on through a small wooden gate in a wall stile. Veer left up to a wall stile and cross the field alongside a wall (L) to the corner of walls and a metal bar gate. Cross this and turn left, following the wall to a wall stile. Turn right through trees and between walls, high (L) and low (R). When you reach the road, turn left. This stretch of

road is steep and feels lengthy, but there is no easy worthwhile alternative route.

5.   At the top turn right into Lady Lane. Almost immediately turn right through a small wooden gate and go down stone steps through the wood. The path goes steadily downhill between the backs of houses. Zigzag left and right on between walls, beside a water channel, over a wall stile, between a wall (L) and fence (R) alongside a wooded valley. On reaching a road, go straight over down Pinedale and through a ginnel between walls, stone (L) and brick (R). Go past an old metal kissing gate at the bottom.

At the driveway, to the right is an impressive residence, Gawthorpe Hall.

6.   Crossing the drive, go through a wall gap and down stone steps and through a metal kissing gate at the bottom. On the tarmac lane pass Beckthorpe Lodge (L). At the road turn right and walk to the junction of roads. Turn left down to Five-Rise Locks. Cross the locks and turn left downhill. Continue on this bank all the way past Three-Rise Locks and under the road bridge. Just beyond this you can turn right through the wall and back to your car.

6: Mortons

The Round of The Glen

Distance: 6.4 km (4 miles) or, with Walk 5, 14.4 km (9 miles)

Time: 2 hours or, with Walk 5, 4½ hours

Map: OS Explorer 288 (1:25 000), Landranger 104 (1:50 000)

Parking: in East Morton, on the main road through the village in a lay-by alongside the Morton Memorial Institute and Post Office, grid reference: 098419

Terrain: field and open moorland, farm track, path and short stretches of road – the first half involves a moderate uphill ascent all the way up to the edge of Ilkley Moor; the middle section is undulating and the final section a gentle descent

Refreshments: at Busfeild (sic) Arms on the main road in East Morton

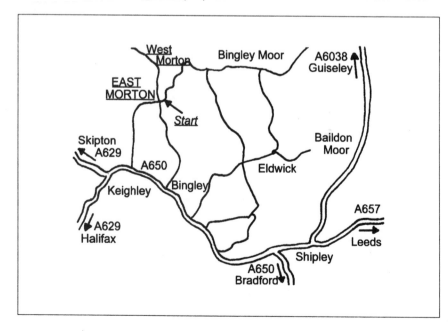

THIS varied walk starts and finishes in the attractive old stone village of East Morton, and takes you up and round by several farms and homesteads. It circles West Morton, a picturesque glen and reservoir on the edge of Rombalds and Ilkley Moors, and gives you extensive views down across the Aire Valley.

Starting with your back to the Memorial Institute and Post Office, cross the road and enter the small 'green' known as Albert's Square. At its top side, go up stone steps and bear, NOT turn, right up a road onto a narrowing gravel track which goes up between walls with a long terrace of stone cottages high up (L). Go on up at the junction of drives, then straight on and to the left of the stone house ahead. Go through a small wooden gate and past the backs of cottages (R). At the top end, use the stone steps and bear left onto a long grass track alongside allotments and between a metal railing (L) and a wall (R). At the far end go over a wall stile and right onto the road.

1. Wind round and just past The Cloisters (L) go through a metal gate (L) and up to the gap. Bear right keeping the wall (L) noting the boulders that form its base. Go up to a metal gate. Cross the field, keeping to the right of a tree; see the large vertical slabs in the wall to the left. Go through a stone pillar stile to the right of two stone pillars (postholes in the left, slot holes in the right). Continue between walls to a metal gate, then straight on to a wall gap. Continue straight on between walls, turning up with the right-hand wall to a metal gate. Go past a barn (L); turn back to view WSW 1913 over the doorway. Go on up right of a metal gate and past Dene Farm (L). As the track bears upwards, see the post-chaise sign of Dene Cottage set in the wall (L).

Author on stepped stile

2.   Just above this and the driveway, turn left, on a path through the fir trees between walls to a small wooden gate. Keep alongside the top of the wall (L) to another small wooden gate plus wall stile. Follow the wall (L) to a wall stile, then round left to another wall stile with stone steps on the far side. Go past the wooden farm gate beside the farm (L). Continue to the tarmac drive. Go straight over the junction past Barn House Farm and other houses/cottages in the row (R).

Along this stretch and higher up you can gain extensive views of the Aire Valley.

3.   After the row and Field House Barn, at the wall end immediately cross the wall stile (R) up a ginnel to a wall stile at the barn end (L). Go on and over a beck, then over a wall stile and follow the wall uphill round to the right. Note how the wall has been built round the tree on the corner. Then veer diagonally left up the field to a wall stile at the top left-hand corner. Over the stile turn right up the wall, veering slightly left steeply up to a stepped stile in mid-wall ahead. Go up between walls and up stone steps, then left onto a terrace in front of cottages. Bear right up a tarmac drive to Ilkley Road. Bear right up to and straight over the crossroads at Street Lane. Near the crest of the road turn right through the metal gate (or kissing gate) onto a bridleway. Go past a house (R) and through a metal gate, and in 20 metres through a small metal gate. Bend right and past a barn (R).

4.   Do NOT go straight on through the gate, but turn left and follow the line of the wall (R). Follow the track as it goes down through a metal gate and over Bradup Beck — view the curved bridge (L), dated 1944. Go up right and round to another metal gate. The track takes you to a succession of gates and alongside a wooded glen (R). You walk through the right-hand of two metal gates, beside a wall (L), then to another gate; the track bends left and right round to cross a stream. Go on through a gate, and further on through another gate with a sheep shelter (R).

Again, you have extensive views of the Aire valley. The reservoir below is the haunt of herons.

5.   Bend left to an open gateway and over a beck. Follow the wall right round to an open gateway with tall stone gateposts. Go under power lines to a gate, then left and through another one. Follow the road right round a half circle down to a metal gate with a cattle grid. Go on into the wood, walking down and over the overflow ladder of Sunny Dale Reservoir. Carry on round left to a metal gate or wooden kissing gate (L).

6.   Walk on down round right to an open gateway and high wall (L). At the junction turn left down Upwood Lane between walls. At the road bear right and up past the cottages of Morton Fold. There is a small graveyard (L) alongside the Methodist Church (1846), now converted. Carry on downhill to the main road.

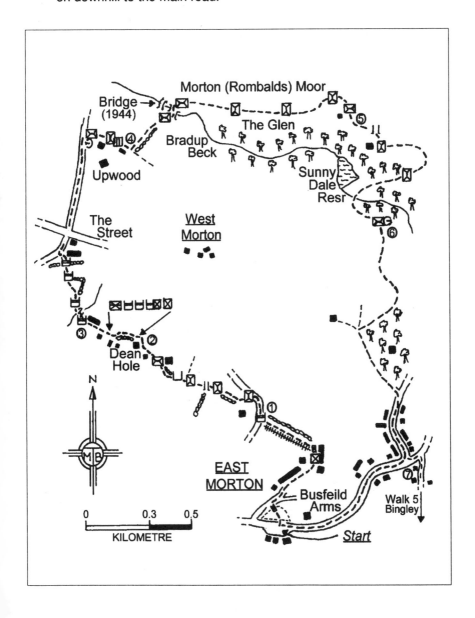

7.   [You can join this walk with Walk 5: turn left for 10 metres, then right into the cobbled Little Lane. Go past Ainsworth's Fold (R), The Barn (L), through a small metal gate, and down a track between walls. At the bottom crossing cobbles past Cliffe House, turn left for 20 metres, then right down a narrow track to cross a metal bridge with railings at the bottom. Go straight on – see Walk 5, point 3].

Continuing on Walk 6, turn right downhill past Sun Street, The Square and Back Lane, and the Busfeild Arms to return to your car – why spelt 'Busfeild'?

7: Eldwick

A Monksway and Becks

Distance: 4.8 km (3 miles)

Time: 1½ hours

Map: OS Explorer 288 (1:25 000), Landranger 104 (1:50 000)

Parking: in Eldwick: either in a lay-by close to the junction of roads on Spring Lane, the road from Baildon Moor, or in the vicinity of The Acorn in The Green, grid reference: 126406

Terrain: field and open heathland, farm track, path and short stretches of road – undulating with only moderate ascents and descents

Refreshments: at The Acorn in The Green

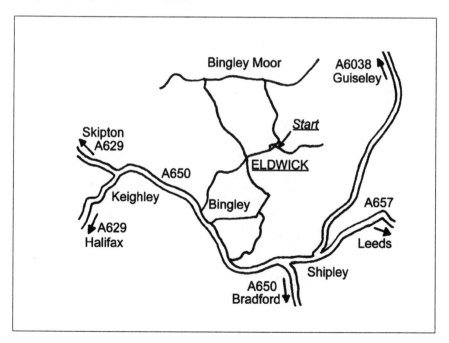

The Monksway

THIS walk is a very pleasant and short stroll over easy walking countryside. It takes you upwards via a former trackway, known locally
as 'The Monksway', and returns you beside and over several becks in
a picturesque glen.

If you have parked in Spring Lane walk straight ahead to the junction.
Turn left over the bridge and in 20 metres turn right into The Green and
up past The Acorn. After bungalows (R) the road becomes a gravel,
then tarmac, track up alongside trees and a beck (R). At the right bend,
turn left up an uneven stony track eventually between walls.

1. Before reaching the top of the track, turn right and go between stone
    gateposts and undulate over a paved trackway, The Monksway —
    where did this go from and to? It takes you over a couple of becks and
    between walls. Use the stepping stones across the overflow from
    Eldwick Reservoir (L), and go up to and through a wooden fence gate
    (or squeeze past its left-hand side). Go up the public bridleway. At the
    road turn right for 80 metres.

    *A little further down is Eldwick Hall. Up left behind you is Eldwick Crag
    on the edge of Bingley Moor.*

2. Go left over a wall stile and up beside the wire fence (R) to a wall stile.
    Walk diagonally right up the field to the right-hand white gate, ignoring
    the wall stile (R), in the top corner. Turn right onto the farm drive. At Mid-
    dle Farm see the barn (R) with its cow weather vane and in front of it a
    large stone with the floral carving of the letters MR. Go left of the farm
    building to a large fence gate, on past the building to a fence stile lead-
    ing through trees to a stepped wall stile (a bit tricky to get over!). Walk
    over the field keeping more or less by the wall (R) to a stepped wall stile.
    Turn right down the farm track and past Moorlands (L).

    *On the Dales Way (Bradford-Ilkley Link) you get a good view of
    Baildon Moor.*

3. Go through a small wooden gate. Walk down the field beside the wire
    fence (R) to a fence stile. Go on shortly past a fence stile against a wall,
    and veer left at a four-way signpost, keeping right of a telegraph pole, to
    another fence stile. Carry on beside a wall (R) to a small fence gate.
    Veer right on a grassy track with a ditch (L) to a fence stile. Go on be-
    tween fences. Zigzag right and left by Golcar Farm on a permissive
    bridleway to a small metal gate. Bear right and down the farm drive
    (halfway down on the left is a stone water trough) and past a bungalow
    (L) with a cock weather vane.

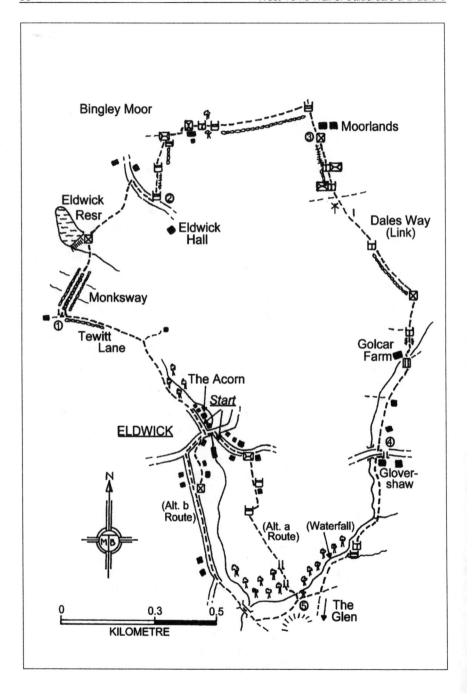

Bingley Moor

Moorlands

Eldwick
Resr

Eldwick
Hall

Dales Way
(Link)

Monksway

Tewitt
Lane

Golcar
Farm

The Acorn

Start

ELDWICK

Glover-
shaw

N

(Alt. b
Route)

(Alt. a
Route)

(Waterfall)

The
Glen

0   0.3   0.5
KILOMETRE

4. Cross Glovershaw Lane at the Eldwick boundary and go through a stone pillar stile, signposted to The Glen. Turn right and left round a barn. Walk on beside a beck (R) and eventually cross a beck flowing from the left. Going right round a tree you pass a small stone pillar (R), with the inscribed letters WTs and Bs. Go on past a small waterfall, where the beck cascades down into the glen. You come to a fence stile, then wall stile and cross a beck flowing in from the left. Shortly go straight on up onto open heathland. At cross-paths turn right and go on down, keeping a former quarry (L) and the stream close to your right.

5. Before a left bend, with an oak sapling (R), you have a choice of routes:

5a) If you prefer the adventurous route and don't mind a bit of a scramble, turn right and find a way down through the ferns to the beck at the bottom. Cross the beck, go over the wall and through wooden posts and up the field to squeeze through a stone pillar stile. Follow the line of the wall (L) up to a wall stile. Turn right by the wall. Note the large blocks in the base of the wall facing you. Turn left alongside this wall and go through a metal gate. Just past a wooden shed/stone building (R) is a blocked wall stile, but you can find your way out of the field at the top through one or other metal gates. Turn left onto Spring Lane and past Spring Farm (BF1772), and return to wherever you have parked your car;

5b) For a more straightforward and easier walking route, carry straight on and down through concrete pillars. At the bottom turn right on a broad track and over a bridge with stone (castellated) parapets. Bear up right on a tarmac path alongside the beck (R) and past Lode Pit Lane (L). Carry on up Saltaire Road. Towards the top you can go through a small gate (R) signposted Lilac Cottage, down steps and up a grassy track, bearing round at the top past a stone house and out onto the road by the bridge.

8: Cullingworth

The Viaduct Walk

Distance: 8.6 km (5½ miles)

Time: 2½ hours

Map: OS Outdoor Leisure 21 (1:25 000), Landranger 104 (1:50 000)

Parking: in the vicinity of St John the Evangelist Church and The George Inn in Church Street, Cullingworth, off B6429 leading from A629 to Harden, grid reference: 067368

Terrain: field and meadow, woodland, path and farm track, and short stretches of road – undulating with moderate ascents

Refreshments: The George, Church Street; The Fleece, Cullingworth Gate

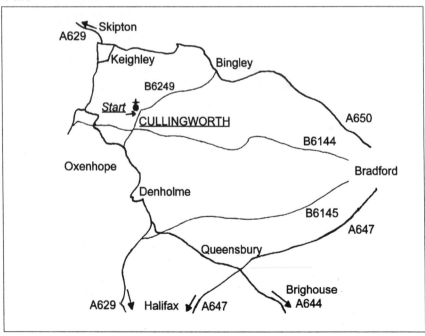

THIS very pleasant walk, starting and finishing in the attractive village of Cullingworth takes you through picturesque wooded valleys, past waterfalls and an impressive viaduct, and gives extensive views from Manywells Height.

Starting in the 'square' facing The George and with the church (L), go leftish down Old Lane past Kaye Hill cottages and over cobbles at its narrowed bottom end. Go left on to the main road (B6429), and into and out of the dip. Opposite Hunters Green (L), you turn right through a wall gap. Go down stone steps and walk by a wall (L), ducking under the bough of a hawthorn bush. Go over a stream, up stone steps and over a wall stile. Go over a tumbledown wall, noting how the wall further on (L) is built on large boulders. The path seems to go down to open ground, BUT go through a wall + wooden pillar stile (L). Go right along the top side of the wall until, going over a wall stile, you follow the wall (L).

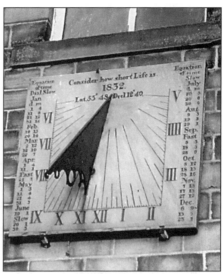

Cullingworth

1. At the corner of the field, turn right down to a metal bridge with railings over the Cow House Beck. Walk up over a tumbledown wall with stone pillar (L) and beside a line of trees. At the top of the field, go up a stepped wall stile and carry straight on up through the woodland.

When, at the top of the woodland, you hear the waterfalls to your left, it is worth taking the time to bear off left to view them, but take care as the path is slippery.

Returning to the path, turn left up a steep bit to a fence stile and out of the wood. Bear left down into the dip, cross a fence stile over a metal railing and turn right. Walk down into a delightful little gorge to cross a substantial bridge with wooden railings. Go straight up, then turn right up stone steps on to a track towards Hewenden.

Beyond Bents Mill, to the right below is a ford, weir and mill race. Further on, the viaduct of a former railway comes impressively into view. Note Hewenden Mill (R) with its weather vane of St George slaying the dragon!

2. Go over a water soakaway and between walls, then up stone steps left of the former Bents Mill. Climb up a steepish slope. At the top of more steps turn right and down a concrete road. At the right bend go straight on through stone pillars, passing a power pole and go right round the edge of a wood. Cross a brook over a plank bridge and go up through a wall stile. Continue along the hillside past pylons (L). Continue on, squeezing between a stone pillar (L) and iron railing (R), and then in/out of/under trees. Go right down steps between wild raspberries and gorse to a stone pillar stile. Cross the field to a wooden pillar stile and onto the road. Turn right down (beware traffic) and over the stream, ignoring both footpath signs (L). Go up the road to the top of the rise.

Going under the viaduct, note the curve on it, built in 1884: 123 ft high with 17 arches – where did this railway start and finish?

3. Turn left over a wall stile on Senior Way. Follow the wall (R) to the right-hand corner, and go right over a wall + fence stile. Go right of a hawthorn bush to a small fence gate with concrete pillars in the right-hand corner, and under the viaduct. Follow the wall (R) round to a fence stile and bear diagonally left to a stone pillar stile beside a metal gate (L). Turn right up alongside the wall (R), keeping left of the barn, to a fence stile in the top right corner. At the farm track, turn right through a metal gate. At the junction turn left behind the farmhouse. Take the right-hand of the two metal gates ahead, following the stony track up right as it winds round a quarry (R). (Do NOT cross the wall stile (R) that leads round to continuous and inpenetrable fences.) Go on through two metal gates with a barn (R). Turn right by a wall (R). Go right through a gate in mid-wall and left alongside the wall. Go through a metal gate.

There are extensive views from Manywells Heights. Manywells Spring is said to be 'one of the most extraordinary springs in the kingdom, its volume computed at above half a million gallons a day.'

4. Turn left up a bridleway past a landfill site (R). At the top end turn left for 50 metres. Cross the road and turn acutely right down a bridleway between walls. Continue down this old trackway past West Manywells Farm (L). After crossing Manywells Beck walk up past Coldspring Mill with its mill shop and tea room (L). Continue up a broad drive past Springfield. Turn left up Haworth Road for 150 metres.

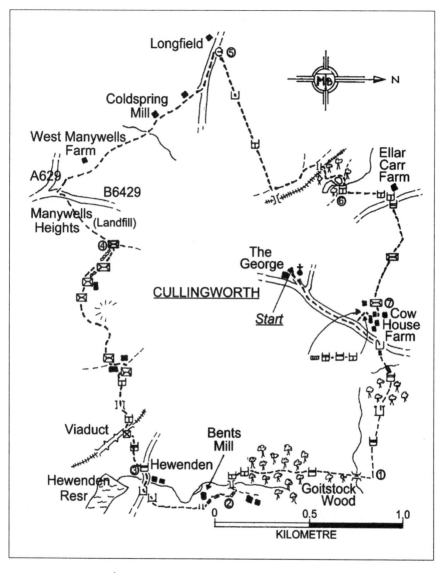

The next part of the route is along a raised trackway; the right-hand wall is well-built with alternate small and large topping stones.

5.   Turn right opposite Longfield (L) through a metal kissing gate. Follow the wall (R) and go through a wall gap. Go on to a fence stile and continue between walls. Just before a railway bridge, turn left on a farm

track. Bear left and right with the track, then veer right through stone gateposts between fences and bushes, and go under a railway bridge. Bear round left and down through trees with a large pond down (R). Fork right and immediately over the stream (Ellar Carr Beck).

6. Turn left over a fence stile and go up between fences. Go over a fence stile and out of the trees, and over an open field to a fence stile through a wall gap. Cross the road, go over a wall stile, alongside a wall (R) and past an open metal gate. Bear right alongside a wall (L). Go through a metal gate and head right past a lone bush and tree. Bend left with a fence (L) to a metal gate.

7. Walk into the hamlet of Cow House Farm. Turn right on the far side of No. 11 and past a building (L), with a horse and rider weather vane, to a fence stile in the right-hand corner. Go down a ginnel and alongside a wall (L) to a wall stile. Walk down the field to a fence + slab stile, and down between walls, over cobbles and down stone steps. Turn right and retrace your steps up the road. Go right up Old Lane to your car in the church 'square'.

9: Harden

Woodlands and Views

Distance: 6.2 km (4 miles)

Time: 2½ hours

Map: OS Landranger 104 (1:50 000), Explorer 288 and Outdoor Leisure 21 (1:25 000)

Parking: in the vicinity of The Malt Shovel on the road between Harden and Wilsden, grid reference: 088378

Terrain: field and meadow, woodland, path and farm track, and short stretches of road – undulating, but with moderately steep and strenuous ascents in the early sections

Refreshments: at The Malt Shovel, (A Heritage Inn), Harden; Garden and Leisure Centre

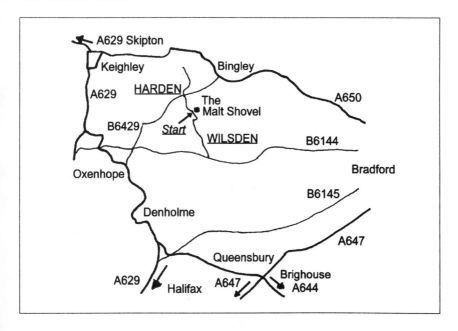

THIS very pleasant walk takes you steadily uphill through woodland and the village of Wilsden. Over the top it gives you extensive views including of a railway viaduct. It returns you down a most picturesque gorge past waterfalls and through Goitstock Wood.

Starting with The Malt Shovel (L) walk uphill veering right up Mill Hill Top ('local access only'). In the interests of safety, when you join the main road, walk up through the car park of the Garden and Leisure Centre. At its top entrance cross the road and go over a wall + fence stile. Go down over the field and cross Wilsden Beck. If the beck is swollen with rain, see the note below. Once across, go up the far bank beside a wall (L) and through a wall gap. Take the track immediately on your right; where it meets the main track, veer right over and alongside a wall (R). Go up through mixed woodland of mainly silver birch and oak. In 100 metres follow the path straight on as it goes upwards gently and eventually steeply leftwards.

[If the beck is uncrossable, retrace steps to the road, turn right and, taking care of oncoming traffic, bend round right downhill. Turn sharp right on Sandy Banks, proceeding over the bridge by the unmade road. Continue straight on up until you reach the wall gap (R).]

1. Passing two rocks (L), at the top turn right onto a level path alongside a wall (L). Squeeze past large rocks and a stone pillar (R). Further on turn right onto a public bridleway. In 50 metres turn left and then bend right over a stream and left up a road between houses in Smithy Lane past Lee Farm (R) and The Smithy (L). At the road turn right. In 50 metres cross and turn left up Moss Row between a former mill (L) and cottages (R). Through the wall, turn left. In 15 metres turn right steeply up a ginnel between walls and out right into Wilsden Hill Road. Walk steeply up between houses.

2. At the far top, alongside No. 45 (L) take the track up left. In 50 metres at the metal gate ahead, cross a wall stile on the right. Follow the wall (L) and go over a stone pillar stile ahead, the left pillar with good posthole slots. Go on to a wooden pillar stile through a wall. Go over the field and through a metal gate, with wooden pillars (L). Follow the wall (L). Go through a gap between walls and follow the wall (R) to go through another wall gap.

From here you gain extensive views back over Wilsden, Harden and to Bingley as well as ahead to a railway viaduct and over to Cullingworth.

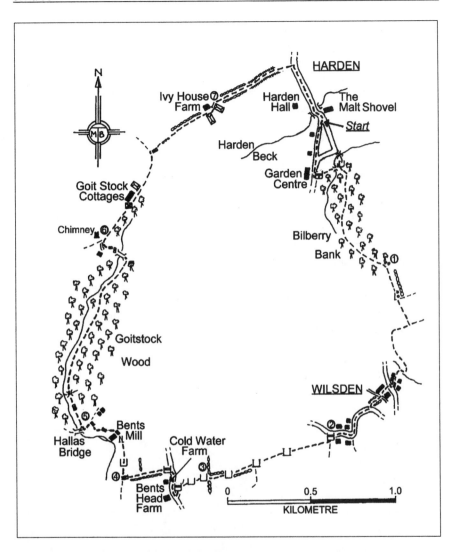

3. Go straight on down and through a wall gap, then down the field to a wall stile. Turn left into a track. In 50 metres at a junction turn right by Bents Hd (sic) Farm and pass Cold Water Farm. Immediately turn left onto a public footpath over a wall stile. Follow down a wall (L) and squeeze between it and a stone pillar/wall end. Then go down further to squeeze again between the wall and a wooden fence end beside a pylon. Go down steps and turn right.

4.   Continue down the hillside and through a wall gap. Go down to cross a brook over a plank bridge. Going round the edge of a wood (L) and passing a power pole, go through stone pillars and up a concrete road. At the top bend, turn left (signposted to Hallas Bridge) down steps and a steepish slope. Go down more stone steps past the former Bents Mill, then between walls and over a water soakaway. Turn left down stone steps and onto a track taking you down to a substantial bridge. Before it turn right onto Senior Way into Goitstock Wood.

The path takes you down a miniature gorge through picturesque woodland, alongside tumbling waterfalls and deep pools.

5.   Go down stone steps and over a plank bridge through the trees. At one point there is a tricky descent with a metal rail to gain a fine view. Continue through the wood and emerge passing a cottage (R). Cross left over a wooden bridge to Leech Lane, and follow the path round onto the lane. Turn left for 20 metres. Turn right up alongside a hedge (L).

6.   Note the old two-stage chimney stack up left. Veer right up through trees. Continue past a wooden gate, the row of Goit Stock Cottages, including Penny Cote (L), and on a tarmac drive past a garage with a cock weather vane. Zigzag past a pillar with a metal gate (L) and on to a roadway. In 100 metres halfway round the bend left, descend stone steps to the right between narrowing fences. Cross over a stream, then go alongside a wall (L) to squeeze between a wall and a farm gate. Go on to Ivy House Farm (L).

Note the plaque that bears the intriguing inscription: 'Never ever underestimate man's ability to feel sorry for himself' – where does that quotation come from?

7.   Bear up left through a metal gate and on between walls, then fences. At the road, the village of Harden is up left, but turn right down past Harden Hall (R) which has a fine wrought iron gate with acorns and SA 1930. Continue to cross the bridge over Harden Beck to wherever you have parked your car.

10: Haworth

A 'different' stroll round Brontë-land

Distance: 6 km (3¾ miles)

Time: 2 hours

Map: OS Outdoor Leisure 21 (1:25 000), Landranger 104 (1:50 000)

Parking: in The Parsonage Museum (pay) car park in West Lane off North Street (B6142) at the top of Haworth, grid reference: 028374

Terrain: field and meadow, path and farm track, and short stretches of road—moderately strenuous in parts with steepish ascents and descents

Refreshments: many places in Haworth

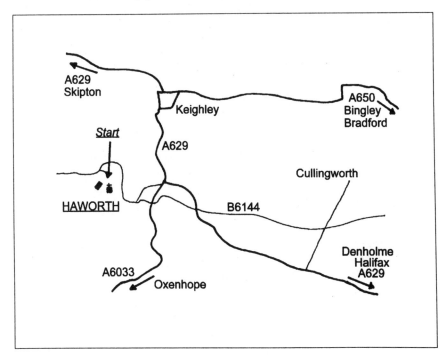

THIS is a 'different' walk around Haworth. It takes you on the north side of Haworth down into the picturesque Worth valley, twice crossing the River Worth. It goes via a number of farmsteads on the opposite hillside before returning past some of the famous sites of interest in the town itself. Special features are hump-back bridges and a variety of small wooden and metal gates.

Haworth: packhorse bridge

Starting with your back to the Parsonage Museum, go left out of the car park back into West Lane. In a few metres turn acutely right into North Street. In about 150 metres, cross the road and, beyond Currer House (1895) on your left, turn acutely left on a footpath past garages (R) and on between walls.

Graveyards: over the wall (L) is a graveyard of the Baptist Church (built MDCCLII – which is what date?) – now tucked in between modern houses; shortly you pass between the graveyards of West Lane Methodist Church.

1.   Go past stone gateposts with a wall (R) and on between narrowing walls to squeeze left of a metal gate over a fence stile. Cross a farm track and go between stone pillars through a fence. Veer right down over a field to

a metal rod stile. Go down a ginnel between walls/fences. Zigzag right and left down steps and through a small wooden gate. Go past a house (L) to a fence stile over a wall with a bush (L). The gully path running down between walls is wettish, so the preferable way is straight down the field, left of the gully, to a fence stile in the bottom.

2. Follow a stream (L) and wall (R) to go left up and over a delightfully scenic packhorse bridge at the confluence of streams with the River Worth. Go right of a wooden gate, to the left-hand fence stile with a metal gate (R). Follow the line of the wire fence (L). Continue for some way alongside the stream (L) as it meanders down over weirs. Go through a wooden gate with barn (R). Go onto a concrete road to a small wooden kissing gate to the right of a concrete bridge.

You now go up a former trackway into an ever deepening gorge with a waterfall at its head.

3. Turn right and go past a hump-back bridge (L) up between stone pillars through woodland over stone slabs beside a wall (R). Zigzag left and right up between fences, again over well-worn slabs and under trees (watch your head!). Go out of the wood through short stone pillars.

4. Turn right and go over a fence stile. Immediately turn left over a fence stile. Do NOT go left up the gully, but go straight over the field towards houses and stone pillars at a wall corner (R). Continue straight on into narrowing walls and squeeze through a small metal gate in the wall. Go alongside a wall (R) to a fence stile. After 50 metres turn left towards houses at Lower Scholes Farm.

5. Turn right in front of the houses, the last one inscribed with 1785 TM (for Thomas Midgley). Go on through metal gates between imposing gateposts. Go straight on left of three trees and alongside a wire fence (L) to a fence + wall stile in the corner between rose bushes. Continue in the same direction to a wall stile, beyond a metal gate (L). Turn right to a small wooden gate in a wall – just before it is a huge block of stone, with a carved arched niche on its far side. Bear left up to the far side of trees and to a wall stile + fence gate. Go straight across the field to a fence stile, and in 20 metres to a wall stile. Green Well Farm is to the right. Turn left up a gravel/concrete track. As it bends left, go right over a wall stile.

6. Walk beside a wall (R) past a fence stile and on to a narrow metal gate, with a fancier one (R). Turn left of and round buildings and where the drive comes in from Lower Hobcote Farm (R), with an anemometer on its roof, go right opposite and through stone pillars. Follow the wall

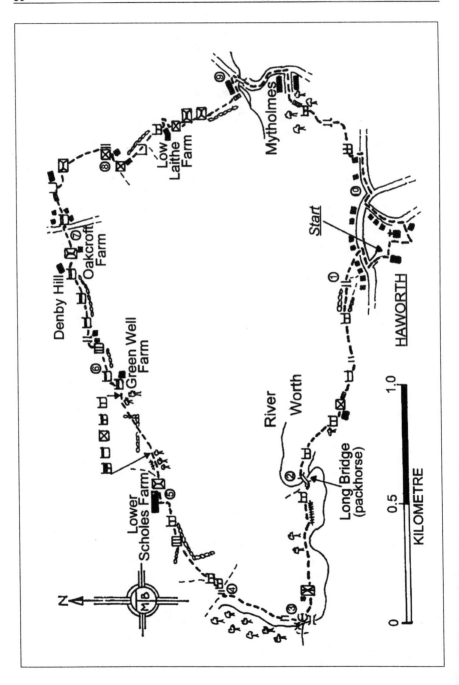

round right. 'Victoria Street' looks incongruous on the garage end! Go on to a well-worn stone stile and a similarly worn one straight on. You come to a wall stile in the corner. Turn right by Denby Hill Farm with weather vanes: (house) shepherd with sheep and dog; (barn end) a fine cock. Go on through stone pillars and metal gate, and between walls; the right-hand one round Oakworth Farm is well 'dressed', including topping stones. Just below it, note the steps down to what may be a covered well.

7. At the road turn right. In 20 metres turn left over a stepped wall stile and go between walls. At the end go down stone steps through a wall. Turn right and follow a dirt track round left. When in front of cottages (L), turn right through a farm gate. The way ahead is indistinct but you need to go down the field, in the direction of the modern windmill across the valley, to the bottom right corner. Go through stone pillars and a small metal gate beside a barn (L).

8. Walk beside a wall (L) through a row of wooden posts. Then immediately go left through a small wooden gate and down stone steps, and follow the wall (L) down. Squeeze through a wall gap and go down, noting a lone chimney (L), to a fence stile in the bottom left corner. Go left of a renovated farmhouse, noting the stone mounting block in front. Go left through stone gateposts, then turn acutely right onto a lane past an old Albion Root Cutter. In 10 metres turn left down cobble setts and through a small wooden gate past stables (L). Go past a metal gate, then follow the wall (R) over slabs round to go between a wooden farm gate and stone pillar. Continue straight on down the field alongside the wall (R). At the bottom go slightly left, then down stone steps on the right-hand side of cottages. Turn left in front of them.

9. At the end of Spring Row, turn right up the road going from Providence Lane to Mytholmes. Cross the river and go uphill until it levels out. Turn right into Baden Street in front of Fir Tree, Hunters Moon and Cedar Cottages with mouse and corn. At the end of the street go between widely spaced poles. Straight on and in 30 metres veer left up through trees, up stone steps and over a fence stile in a wall. Continue in the same direction up the field and over a tumbledown wall. Turn left and go through stone gateposts and up between walls. Veer right up between sheds and zigzag through a wooden gate. Turn left on a lane to a road. Turn right and go up past the black and white Bankda'm (1645), with a sundial inscribed GF+ACF. Turn right into North Street.

10. Almost immediately turn left along Changegate into the village of Haworth. Go past Updown Cottage (L) and the Old White Lion (R).

At the junction, you may care to walk down the cobbled street to your left; to your right is the Kings Arms, opposite is the Black Bull, frequented by Bramwell Brontë; straight on is St Michael and All Angels Parish Church.

Go up on the left side of the church and before steps turn right with the Parsonage over the wall (L) and out onto the street. Turn left and pass (R) the school, built 1832, where Charlotte Brontë taught. Opposite the Parsonage Museum, turn right through stone gateposts into the car park.

11: Oxenhope

The Walk round the 'Enclosure'

Distance: 7.6 km (4¾ miles)

Time: 2½ hours

Map: OS Outdoor Leisure 21 (1:25 000), Landranger 104 (1:50 000)

Parking: in the car park near Oxenhope Station and Museum, off A6033, grid reference: 032353

Terrain: field and moorland hillside, path and farm track, short stretches of road – moderate ascents on the first half, undulating, descending and level thereon

Refreshments: several in Oxenhope

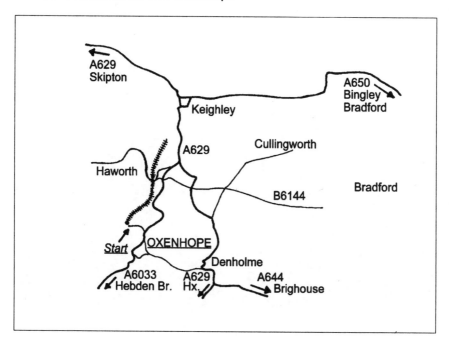

THIS is a pleasant and varied walk. It starts by taking you through some of the older parts of Oxenhope, then takes you up high and affords you extensive and fine views across the valley as far as Haworth, before returning you alongside the Keighley and Worth Valley railway.

Starting with the station to your left walk eastwards and up Mill Lane, crossing the river. Continue into Harry Lane; note at the top the house (R) has a metal doored coal bunker, set in the wall. Turn left onto A6033 and immediately right up Dark Lane between ivy-clad walls. As it levels out turn right past Acorns (L) and further on pass Eastville Cottages (R).

As you descend past a barn/garage (R), note in the wall (L) a fountain inscribed JW 1859; interestingly the water flows out of the stone trough at the right-hand side. At the bottom of the lane you are entering Lower Town, an old part of Oxenhope, and there is another JW (1856) inscribed trough (R). Further on in Yate Lane, opposite Farra Street, on your right is a 17th -century house with a 'period' mansion on its far end. What are the meanings of 'Yate' and 'Farra'?

Oxenhope: Yate Lane

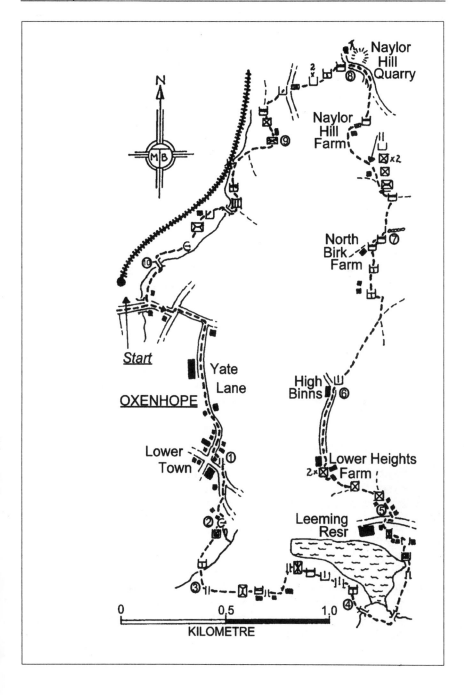

1. Turn left into Farra Street, past the backs of cottages and through stone pillars. At the road (Station Road) continue. In 60 metres, as the road turns left uphill into Denholme Road, it passes between the two halves of the Wesleyan Lower Town Old Burial Ground, AD 1808-1907. Go straight over into Jew Lane. On your right is a former mill, refurbished into apartments, but still with its pond. Go uphill, and where it levels out, before the left bend and the road fork into Back Leeming, veer right onto a public footpath. Go down between walls. Bear left in front of Wadsworth House on a gravel lane, bending right, with a pond (L), and up past Bull Hill.

2. Go through a small wooden kissing gate and up the fence with a pond (L). Take stone steps through a wall and small wooden gate, with a farm gate (L) complete with poles in its slot holes. Go uphill, not up right but keeping close to the stream (L). Nearly in the top corner turn left to cross the stream and then a fence stile. Continue straight on up the slope. Keep to the right-hand and higher path over slabs, going over a conduit from the reservoir. Take care, as the ground hereabouts can be very wet. Continue up in the same direction to stone steps and a wooden pillar stile.

3. The path takes you uphill, diagonally right past wooden posts, and beside a fence (R) and through a metal farm gate. Go on to cross a wall stile. Walk in front of Berry Lower Isle Farm (R), with a sundial (L) and a large stone lintel over the barn doorway (R). Going through stone gateposts, cross a lane and squeeze past a metal gate (L). Pass cottages (R). Before the next cottage with a dog weather vane on its outhouse, veer left down a cobbled and gravel track towards Leeming Reservoir. Going through gateposts, turn right through a wooden farm gate. Through the next gate veer left beside a fence (L) and over a stepped wall stile. Go through a wall gap with metal pillar, alongside a wall (R) and on through a pillar stile and through a wall + fence stile. You gain a fine view of a converted mill across the reservoir.

4. Follow the wall (L) down and round to a wooden bridge with railings. Go over the stream, down stone steps and up the field. In 50 metres join a track veering left and round the right side of trees. Turn left over a stone bridge, noting the stream conduited between well-built walls. Walk on a track between low walls of different constructions, with rounded toppings. Carry on over open ground with a large mound (L) and through stout gateposts. Go on between higher walls past the head of the reservoir. Turn left up past more gateposts and over a fence stile + small fence gate. Go on between a fence (L) and an old metal railing (R), between walls, small stone pillars, Sykes House and Barn. Turn left along the front of the buildings and through a wooden farm gate. At a fork bear left and through gateposts to go right up a lane (Sykes Fold) and past the Baptist School 1863 (L).

5. At the top turn right passing a milk churn shelf in the wall (R). In 20 metres turn acutely left up a cobbled lane past cottages, including No. 12, 'Longmetre' (!). At the end of the houses (Tansy End) go straight on through a small wooden gate between stone pillars. Go across a field with wall (L) past an old wall stile and squeeze past a wall pillar. In 30 metres go through a fence gate and bear left on a tarmac lane. At the farm ahead bear left down concrete steps. Go right and left down more steps, and through a small fence gate. Turn right alongside a wall and in 15 metres go through a small fence gate and between buildings. Lower Heights Farm (L) has a cock weather vane. Follow the lane gently round right. There is a good view over Oxenhope (L).

6. Opposite a derelict building (L), take a track veering right up between walls. Squeeze through a stile with a metal pillar and go up the track by a wall (L). Follow the higher track through gorse and heather. Good views. Take care here to choose the correct path: when the track starts to get steeper and the wall goes straight on to a fence, turn left downhill; keep going through the heather and gorse until you are just at the end of some holly bushes. Cross the fence stile (R), and keep going down by the fence (L). Cross the track and go beside a fence/wall (L) to a fence stile (L) and metal guard fences. Down left is North Birk Farm with mullion-type windows. Veer left of holly bushes straight to a wall stile. Turn right up the Worth Way between walls and over a wall stile.

7. Veer left with the fence/wall (L) and squeeze between a wooden gatepost and wall (R). Cross a field and a tumbledown wall. Bend gently round right under wires to a wall stile. Turn left down a tarmac track and go straight on through a metal gate. Bear right through a small wooden gate and go along to two more gates. Cross a lane and go through a fence gap, past a shed (L) and by a wall (R). Going through a stone pillar stile (R), go acutely right. Bend round left and beside a wall/fence (L). Bend right round Duck Cottage. Turn acutely right up stone steps and through a stone slab stile. Bend left and go on to a tarmac road. Facing you is a modern windmill above a quarry.

8. Bend left and before the right bend, cross a wall stile straight ahead. Go steeply down the field alongside a wall (L) to a fence stile and then a fence gap, followed by a wall gap and down stone steps. Cross the road diagonally left. Go through a wall gap and bear left down the track. At

the bottom turn left through a well-worn stile. Walk beside a wall (L) to a small wooden gate. Bear up left, then veer right in front of a house.

9. Immediately beyond a wooden farm gate, turn right down a path to the riverside. Pass a hump-back bridge (R). Continue on the river bank, over planks across a brook to a wall stile + zigzag fence stile. Go up stone steps and through a small metal gate + stone pillar stile. Go straight on and turn right, crossing the river on a metal bridge with railings. Turn left along the track with pond (R), and over slabs through a wall gap. Go through a metal gate beside a sewage farm (R). Just before a bridge (L), take a metal kissing gate straight on with the Keighley and Worth Valley Railway over the wall (R).

10. Cross left over the bridge and turn right towards Oxenhope. Go on through a wall gap. You come out into Harry Lane, opposite The Barn, with an inscription to Rt Hon Earl Wilton, 1822, in a high-up niche. Turn right returning to wherever you have parked your car.

Oxenhope: the original name was 'Oxennop' and 'nop' is an old name for 'enclosure'. This explanation may help you with the 'Yate' and 'Farra' question.

12: Tong

Three Walks around Tong

Map: OS Explorer 288 (1:25 000), Landranger 104 (1:50 000)

Parking: in the vicinity of The Greyhound, grid reference: 222307

Terrain: meadow and field, woodland, farm track, path and stretches of road – the walks are undulating with moderate ascents and descents

Refreshments: at The Greyhound in Tong village

Walk (a): Holme and Cockers Dale

Distance: 12 km (7½ miles)

Time: 3½ hours

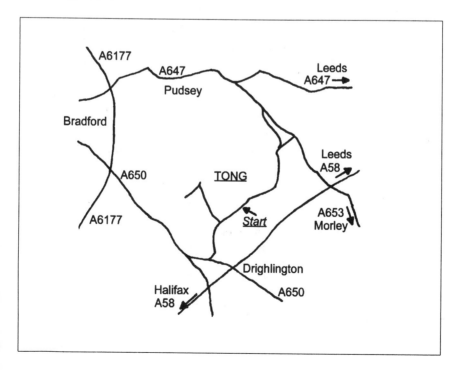

THIS walk is the longest in the Bradford area, starting and finishing in Tong Village. It describes a full circle westwards via the hamlet of Holme before climbing up high and descending through a delightful woodland by a stream below the ridge of the Moravian settlement at Fulneck. On the way back the route goes through another stretch of woodland in Cockers Dale before ascending back to Tong. The special feature of this walk is the V-shaped fence stiles.

Starting with The Greyhound on your right walk up the main street in a south westerly direction past Roma's Cottage and Cobble Lee (L) and the Old Vicarage (R). In front of St James Church — with stone vases on its tower — note the stocks (R) and the horse mounting steps (L); also the impressive gateposts of Tong Hall (R). Carry on until you turn right into New Lane. Go all the way down the lane, in and out of the dip, and on up past the farm (R).

1. At the bottom of the lane, on a left-hand bend, go straight over a V-shaped fence stile. Veer right down to cross a stream on planks and on up to another V-fence stile. Follow the lane up and round to the left. Just before Maythorne Farm, turn left over a slab wall stile and go across the field to a zigzag fence stile. Go left alongside a fence (L) and through a wooden pillar stile, with metal gate (L). Shortly at a post (R), bear down right and alongside the erstwhile pond of Charles Pit (disused). Eventually go over a V-fence stile (R) and turn left alongside a fence (L) to another V-fence stile.

2. Cross the stream to the left bank and go up round the left side of a hollow to a V-fence stile, then bear left up to another. Continue uphill alongside a gully (L) to a V-fence stile. The path takes you up past trees and hawthorn bushes to a V-fence stile. Follow the hedge (L) to a fence stile, then go between hedges and through a gap onto the road.

3. Turn right down the lane past Holme Farm and Barn (R), and into the bottom past Holme Village. Then turn right with the lane. The lane bends left and goes uphill. As it bends left again, take the public footpath to the right over a V-fence stile. Go between fences to a fence stile. Carry straight on up the field keeping to the right of hawthorn bushes for a fence stile beside a bush in the top corner of the field.

4. Go right round the bushes onto a broad track and take the left fork. Before you enter the trees, veer left onto a path into the wood with the stream (R) until you cross it. Keep up to the right to join the main track. Keep to this track as it goes gently downhill for a considerable distance.

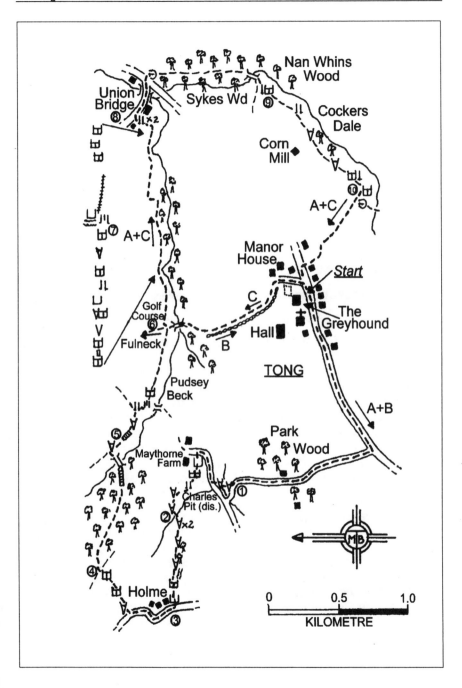

Eventually you go more steeply down over widely-spaced wooden steps. At the bottom, cross the stream via a stone bridge. At the cross-paths go over a V-shaped wooden bridge with railings, down stone steps and veer right onto a path which follows the stream (R) as it meanders. You are now on the Leeds Country Walk (LCW + Owl Sign).

5.   Go over wooden steps, stone slabs and a V-fence stile. Where the path goes off left, flagged further up, veer right to a wooden pillar stile. Go right and over slabs to three stone pillars (L). Do NOT go over the bridge, but turn left over a fence stile. Go over the field generally keeping to the right of bushes to the corner of the golf course (R). Go between pillars, wood (L) and stone (R), and beside the stream (R), sometimes over stones and up/down steps.

6.   At the cross-paths and golf course crossing, with the Moravian settlement of Fulneck up left:

Who were/are Moravians?

Walk (B) goes off right and over a metal bridge (see below for end);

Walk (C) (see below for start) comes in from the right.

Walks A and C continue straight on keeping the golf course on your left. At the bend there is a warning to beware of golfers and balls ahead. At the end go left of the tee and over a fence stile and slab over a stream. Go on to a fence stile with a fence (L) and then to a V-fence stile with fence (R). Continue to another V-fence and usual fence stile together. A short stretch between fences brings you to a wall gap. Glimpse Fulneck School (L). Veer right to go between wooden pillars, then alongside the stream to a fence stile and between wire fences. Be careful along this stretch as it can be very muddy, and the path is crumbling away. Go to a V-shaped wall stile, and veer left past fences, some possibly broken, to another fence stile.

7.   The easiest way to proceed is to go straight ahead to a broken wooden post between old gateposts. Turn sharp left between broken wooden posts and uphill alongside a hedge (L) and through a gap in the fence. Turn right beside a fence (R). Continue until almost the end, then bear slightly left to a fence stile below trees by the bend of the stream. Go alongside the bank to a fence stile and across the meadow to another fence stile. Bend left with the stream, then round right by a wall (L). Then turn left up through metal posts and then wooden posts between walls to the road.

8.   Turn right into Roker Lane and past various works and over a bridge at

the confluence of streams (R). At the T-junction go straight over onto a public footpath directing you to Sykes' Wood. Immediately go through the wooden kissing gate (R) and follow the path downhill into the woodland. Eventually you will come to a wooden bridge with metal railings (R). Cross the stream and veer up left and under trees to a fence stile with a 7ft stone pillar (R).

9. Go alongside the trees, sometimes on stone flags, and through wide stone gateposts. Cross a V-fence stile and go over a couple of soakaways. On the right of the second there is a little waterfall tumbling over a rock face. Carry on, keep to the left, and come to a V-fence stile and then another fence stile beside metal pillars (L). Next, there is a fence stile at the junction of paths.

10. Turn right, ignore the kissing gate (L) and carry straight on up a track (Springfield Lane) between fences overgrown with trees. Go past imposing gateposts (R), and over a slab pavement in parts. The track widens out and bends left, then right, up to the road. Turn left and pass on your right a cottage (no. 37) with a witch weather vane. Return to where you have parked your car.

Walk (B): Tong and Holme

Distance: 8 km (5 miles)

Time: 2½ hours

THIS is a shorter version of Walk (A), following the route Walk (A) round to the golf course. It then turns south over a metal bridge and takes you up a former flagged trackway ascending back to Tong. The special feature of this walk is the V-shaped fence stiles.

Follow the route of Walk (A) until:

6. At the golf course crossing Walk (B) goes off right and over a metal bridge with railings and through wooden posts to go up a former flagged trackway. The track goes up quite steeply in places and you get glimpses of the rear of Tong Hall (R). Continue up alongside the wall (R). Bend left and then right into Keeper Lane, passing Keeper Cottage and The Manor House (L). At the main road turn right. On your right is Pinfold, where stray animals were kept until claimed by their owners, and an old water fountain, dated AD 184?, with water troughs on its left. Return to wherever you have parked your car.

Walk (C): Tong and Cockers Dale

Distance: 6 km (3¾ miles)

Time: 2 hours

THIS is the shortest of the Tong routes starting and finishing in the village of Tong. The walk describes a circle heading northwards and down a former flagged trackway into the valley with the Moravian Settlement of Fulneck up on the opposite ridge. The route turns eastwards along the valley bottom before going through the delightful woodland valley of Cockers Dale and ascending back to Tong. A special feature of this walk is the V-shaped fence stiles.

Starting with The Greyhound on your left walk to the Keeper Lane. At its corner look to your left at the water troughs, a water fountain dated AD 184?, and Pinfold, where stray animals were kept until claimed by their owners. Turn left down Keeper Lane and pass The Manor House and Keeper Cottage (R). Take the path left round the wall to the left and down over a flagged pavement, a former trackway. At the corner of the stream (L) go through wooden posts, up and over a metal bridge with railings. At the golf course with the Moravian Settlement of Fulneck up on the ridge ahead, do NOT go straight on to the course, but turn right.

Now, refer to Walk (A) and follow its route from point 6 (see above) to the end.

Stocks outside Tong church

13: Gauxholme

Water, Water, Everywhere

Distance: 8.4 km (5¼ miles)

Map: OS Outdoor Leisure 21 (1:25 000), Landranger 103 (1:50 000)

Time: 3 hours

Parking: anywhere in the first half mile on or off A681, from where it leaves A6033 from Todmorden at Gauxholme, grid reference: 927232

Terrain: path, farm track, field and open moor/heathland, with short stretches of road; strenuous in parts with moderately steep ascents and quite a hard trek over moorland in the middle of the walk

Refreshments: not available on the walk, but several in Todmorden

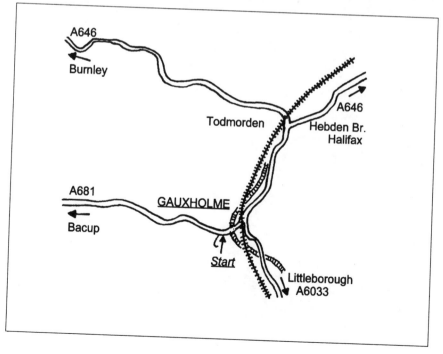

Locks under the railway bridge on the Rochdale Canal

THIS is a walk which takes you past some picturesque surprises. It starts by taking you high up above the Rochdale Canal, in the middle past hidden waterfalls, and after a high level walk over moorland returns you down a delightful clough, before affording you extensive views across to Stoodley Pike. Note: take a compass with you.

Over the first part of the walk view the Rochdale Canal, the railway and the road as they jostle for space in the valley below.

You need to find a small side road, Naze Road, left off the first bend beyond (west of) the canal bridge on A681. Go down this road and over the river, with a cascading waterfall (R). Turn left up through a metal gate to a small wooden gate. Turn acutely right through a metal gate and up a terrace track. Wind your way left up over cobble setts and past two sets of stone gateposts, with slot and postholes (R). Walk up beside a fence/wall (L).

1. Go left over a fence stile towards Law Hey Farm, which provides B+B; note its lanterns and wagon wheels. Go on to the concrete drive. Carry on until at a left bend the concrete becomes gravel. At that point bear off right on a signposted footpath over a beck, and left up beside a wall (R) to a fence stile. Go alongside the wall (R) and trees to a fence stile. Walk along a terrace overlooking the railway, road and canal, and go down leftish to a fence stile, with successive steps at right angles to one another!

2. Turn right up alongside a wall (L) and brook (R) over cobble setts. Veer left with the wall and wind your way up steeply on a somewhat overgrown path. Zigzag right and left past a line of power poles, and turn left at the top alongside a wall (R). Note the stone gatepost with postholes in the wall alcove. Keeping to the top of the wood, you emerge onto a lane.

On your left is a view of the church across the valley. Across the lane is a 'period' house, Nicklety, with three storeys of mullion-type windows, the middle window in the row being larger than the others.

3. Go through a small wooden gate, across the house side garden, and up a gravel path to two fence stiles. Walk alongside a fence (L) to a fence stile, then beside a wall (L) to a fence stile in a wall gap. Turn right up the grassy track and through a metal gate. Continue up between walls, the right-hand one being based on some large rocks, and over a fence stile. Walk beside the wall (R) to a fence stile, with a white farmhouse/equestrian centre (R). Over the stile it looks a daunting prospect down into a deep valley, but the reward comes later! Zigzag downhill through a

metal gate, and all the way down to another metal gate alongside Walsden Works. Through the gate, turn left and zigzag through the works. Where the road beyond the buildings bends left, go straight on up stone steps. Turn right up a road and past the works (R). At a pond continue along its left bank and on to a wooden gate.

4. Wind your way round, high above the stream (R), until you come to a series of waterfalls (the reward!). The first one is actually a weir, but it is not advisable to cross over the coping stones as there is a 5m. vertical drop on one side! Instead, go some metres beyond on the left bank to a small sluice gate below a (natural) waterfall, where there is a safe and easier crossing point, with a more rewarding spectacle. Return on the opposite bank over and under fallen trees, until opposite the weir turn acutely left up the steep slope. Cross a beck on a wooden plank. Down left is the waterfall where you crossed, and another is seen at the next bend. Go on to a fence stile, from where can be seen a further waterfall down left by Ragby Bridge. Turn acutely right up the track and round left to a fence stile and wooden gate. Go on up and through a wooden gate and between a house (Thorus Greece) and a farm.

5. Cross a cattle grid, then turn left onto Foul Clough Road. At the top of the road rise, alongside a new bungalow and derelict cottage (L), you can either:

6a. Turn right onto the open moorland, but take care as the ground is 'infested' with tussocks, separated often by hidden pools – leg breakers! There is no clear path across the moor, but go generally in a north west direction, eventually descending gently to the north east wall of Gorpley Reservoir; or

6b. Head along the road further for the line of pylons, and turn right following them all the way to the reservoir; the terrain is better underfoot until the last 200 metres, and you should not get lost!

Coming to a wooden farm gate (L), go across the overflow of the reservoir, and turn right down a track past the water board buildings. The inscription states that the first sod was dug in May 1900 and the water turned on in March 1905.

There follows the surprise reward for all that tough walking across the moor. As you walk down the delightful Gorpley Clough, note the many waterfalls, a low rock wall (L) draped with moss, lichen and fern, and further down the high, nearly vertical valley side (L), with rocky outcrops, ferns and precariously perched trees.

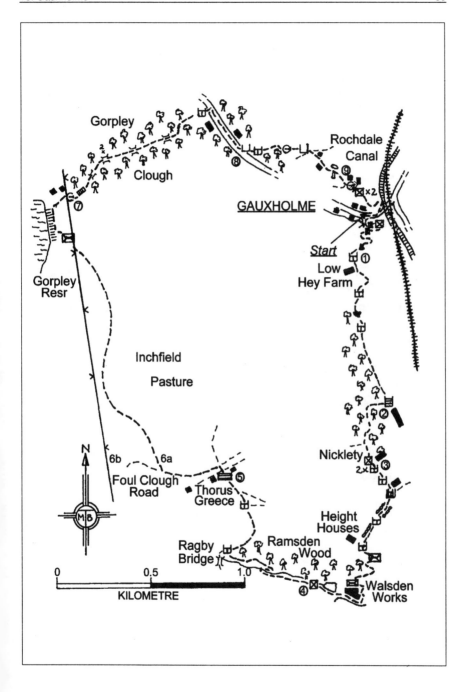

7. Opposite the ornamental gateway go through a metal kissing gate (R) and turn left down to Gorpley Clough. Go down stone steps at various intervals. Further on, zigzag right and left down wooden steps and cross a wooden bridge. Continue up and down wooden steps and across two wooden bridges. Cross another wooden bridge to the right-hand bank, and on down stone steps beside a waterfall (L). Go on down stone steps by another waterfall (L). Cross to the left bank on a wooden bridge. Zig-zag up steps with a stone abutment, and alongside a wall, then fence (R) to a fence stile. At the main road turn right. Pass a 'period' house (L).

8. In 120 metres cross the road, go through a wall gap and up stone steps right to a fence stile. Walk steadily uphill through the trees, cross a stream in a gully and go to a metal kissing gate. Continue on a terrace and through a wall gap with a stone gatepost (R) with three slot holes. Veer right past a power pole and go on and through stone gateposts. At this junction of paths, go straight on past a derelict building and two stones troughs (L), and a farmhouse (R), and down a concrete road. There is a pond (L) and a preserved stone chimney (R).

9. At a right-hand bend, follow the grassy track straight on to a wooden kissing gate. Go down steps past a house (L), Hill View, between fences and through a metal gate. Cross the track to a small wooden gate. Below (R) is a row of cottages with 'middens'. Go to another wooden gate. Walk down beside a wall (R). There is a good view across to Stoodley Pike and of locks on the Rochdale Canal as it goes under the railway. Turn acutely right onto Pexwood Road, and return to wherever you have parked your car.

When you reach the main road (A681), you may care to cross it and view Gauxholme Highest Lock 24. From here you can walk beside the canal under the road towards Todmorden to view the series of locks and the elaborately built railway bridge with its mock castellations, shields, etc.

What is the origin of the names: Gauxholme, Naze, Gorpley and Pexwood?

14: Mankinholes

To Lumbutts Mill and Back

Distance: 9.6 km (6 miles)

Map: OS Outdoor Leisure 21 (1:25 000), Landranger 103 (1:50 000)

Time: 3 hours

Parking: in either of the lay-bys on A646, one with picnic tables, about 1 mile east of Todmorden and 3½ miles from Hebden Bridge; or in Haugh Road, on the west side of Lobb Mill Chandlers, grid reference: 953246

Terrain: path, track, field and open heathland, with short stretches of road; level start and finish along the Rochdale Canal, with a steep ascent and descent, and a long level stretch in the middle below Stoodley Pike

Refreshments: at the Rose and Crown on A646, or halfway round at The Top Brink Inn in Lumbutts

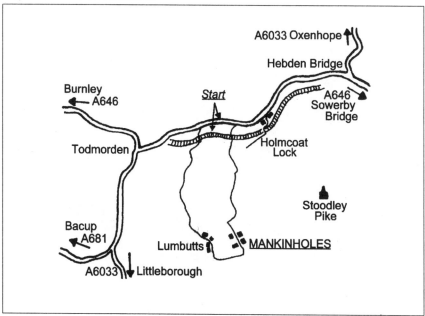

THIS walk contains a variety of walking and points of interest. It starts along and above the Rochdale canal, followed by a steepish ascent up through a wooded glen and out onto open heathland below Stoodley Pike. This level stretch gives you extensive views down into and across the valleys. You walk through the picturesque hamlet of Mankinholes and pass a mill water wheel tower in Lumbutts. The way down is through another wooded glen, before you return beside the canal.

Starting on Haugh Road turn left under the bridge past a chandler's (L) and Lob(b) Mill Lock. Walk along the canal bank until you cross a cobbled overflow close to Shawplains Lock. Continue along the canal bank and go on past a boat builder's (L) and moored craft. The towpath becomes a narrow causeway between the canal and river (L). Pass a milepost (L): Manchester 24; Sowerby Bridge 8, with a memorial plaque, and go on past a tiny cricket ground (L) and a fine terrace of stone houses (R). Continue under a bridge and on over another overflow on stepping stones and boards.

As you walk along the terrace in the next woodland, view the canal, river, main road and a busy railway line, jostling for space in the valley bottom.

A milepost on the Rochdale canal

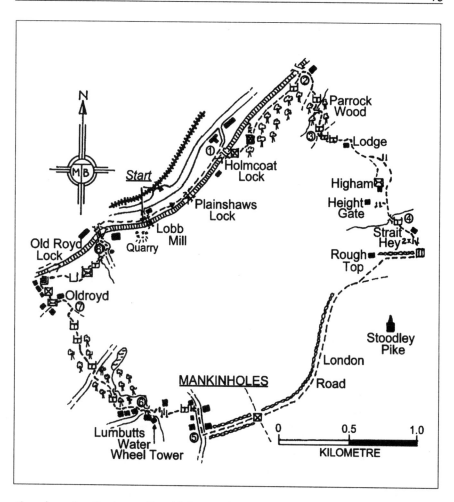

1.   Leaving the towpath at Holmcoat Lock, cross the canal and bear left into Burnt Acres Wood. Go through a small fence gate, up and along the path to two small fence gates on either side of a wall gap. Bear slightly left downhill and then along a level terrace. Go over a fence stile at the far end. Walk downhill to the bridge.

2.   Turn right up the tarmac lane past a metal gate and cottages (L) to an open gate. Veer left and into a woodland glen to a fence stile, with a stream (L) in a deep gully. Go up to and cross left over the stream, then up round to the right under holly bushes. The path is indistinct, but wind your way up until you follow a wall (L) to a fence stile in the top corner.

Go straight on up a farm track for a few metres, then turn left over a fence stile.

3. Go steeply up a field containing young trees to a fence stile. Continue straight on up alongside a fence and hawthorn bushes (L). Bear left round the farmhouse (The Lodge), following a fence round right at the top corner. Then bear left up a grassy track past trees (R) to a stone post under a large holly bush (L). Continue up a wide grass track to the left of a line of hawthorn bushes with a farm track down to the right. Pass between stone gateposts and follow the track round to the right until at a wall it meets a track coming up from the right. Bear left alongside the wall to a metal gate. Through the gate go down a sunken path, originally between walls. Stoodley Pike is in view directly ahead. At a post (L) the right of way veers diagonally left and soon down between walls and gateposts to cross a bridge over a stream to a fence stile.

Stoodley Pike is a 'Peace Monument' (1815). After collapsing in a gale, it was rebuilt in 1856, and is a notable landmark from every direction. Along the next stretch, you get fine views over and across Todmorden.

4. Veer left up to a ruined house on a track which stands slightly proud. The house (Strait Hey) still has the remnants of King beams. Carry on alongside a wall (L) and through two sets of stone gateposts, the second set with three slot holes (R) up to a metal gate. Through the gate, turn right alongside a wall (R) towards Rough Top. Where the power lines cross, follow their line upwards until you join a stony track. Follow this track (called 'London Road', no less! – why?) for a considerable way alongside a wall (R), castellated in places, and intermittent fence. Go through a fence gate beside a farm gate (L), and on between widely spaced walls.

The houses in Mankinholes, mentioned in the Domesday Book, were built facing south to catch as much daylight as possible for the handloom weavers.

5. At the road turn right into the picturesque hamlet of Mankinholes, passing a line of stone water troughs at Moor Edge (R). The house 'Mankinholes' (L) has a witch and cat weather vane. Walk down to the Youth Hostel (R). Turn left before 'The Barn' through stone gateposts with slots and holes. Go over stone slabs to a fence stile. Continue down over slabs alongside a substantial wall (R) to a three-pillar stone stile and down stone steps. Turn right and pass The Top Brink Inn, then left down a bridleway over slabs, then cobbles. At the road, opposite

you in a 'hanging valley' is the Water Wheel Tower of Lumbutts Mill, with the mill race alongside the road to the left. Turn right, go over the bridge, and just up from it, veer right before the first house.

6. Go left down the back of the houses. Follow the wall (R), then bear down right between walls into a wooded glen. The stream (R) cascades down waterfalls until it disappears underground. Go to a fence stile + wooden bridge, with a rock face and waterfall up left. Wind your way up and round to the road, where there is a seat (R) overlooking New Mill Dam — once a mill lodge, now a fishery for anglers — down in the bottom (R). Turn right and walk down for 80 metres. Go left up stone steps to a fence stile and back into the wood. Wind your way round, up and down, out of the wood and cross a fence stile over a wire fence. Go alongside a wire fence (R) to a fence stile, then on and past garages (R) to a lane.

7. Turn left up to a junction, passing the impressive 17th century frontage of a house (R). Turn right through a metal gate and down a track along a wall (R) to a small fence gate. Cross Stone Church is high on the hillside opposite. Descend between a wooden fence (L) and wall (R). Turn right through a wall gap + small fence gate. Head across the field parallel to the canal and Old Royd Lock (L). Go over the foundations of a wall and veer right to a wall gap (R) between stone posts. Go through a gateway with a tall wooden post (L) and bend left to a fence stile (R) beside a stream. Cross a stone slab bridge, go alongside a wall (L) and on between walls past a cottage (L). Go straight on up onto a road and past a mill chimney and derelict mill (R).

8. Bend left over a canal bridge and turn right down steep steps, some with inserts, onto the towpath. Go on past the mill (1832) and further on a disused quarry (R), to wherever you have parked your car.

The flagged paths which criss-cross the hills are called 'causeys'; they connected the villages for trade in finished pieces of cloth.

15: Todmorden

The Calder High View – The Outcrops Walk

Distance: 10 km (6¼ miles)

Map: OS Outdoor Leisure 21 (1:25 000), Landranger 103 (1:50 000)

Time: 3 hours

Parking: off A646, in a public car park (Ashenhurst Road), in front of the Hare and Hounds, grid reference: 930250

Terrain: path, farm track, field and open heathland, with short stretches of road; moderately steep ascent at the beginning and descent at the end, with undulating terrain in the middle mainly over general heathland at high level

Refreshments: the Hare and Hounds, the House That Jack Built, (both on A646) and several in Todmorden

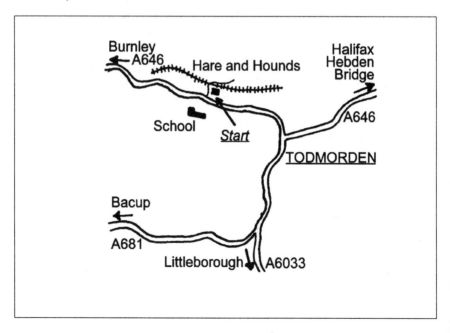

THIS walk starts in the valley bottom and rises through woodland to a generally level section across open heathland, close to craggy outcrops. You gain extensive views over the Calder and Todmorden to Stoodley Pike. You return past a succession of fine 17th century farmhouses, a golf course and quarry workings. Special features of the walk are the high fence stiles, i.e. with several rungs, and combination stiles, e.g. fence plus wall.

Starting from the car park, turn right (west) onto A646 and walk for some 300 metres. Opposite Scaitcliffe Hall turn right into Stoney Royd Lane and go up alongside a brook (L). When the lane becomes a gravel track, go straight on up under trees alongside playing fields (L). Pass on its right a house ahead with the initials SR on its ornate gates, and go alongside the high wall (L). Veer right under a high railway tunnel and up round left and past a stone trough (R). Bend left to walk up in front of Stannally Farm standing up high (R). Bend up right with the main track between walls and through woodland over variously stone and brick, pavings and cobbles, and with waterfalls (R and L).

1.   At the top you come to a wooden kissing gate on the right of a farm gate. Go through the gate, then turn left alongside a fence (L) to go over a brook to a small metal gate, and left up to another one. Turn right alongside the wall (R) and past a sheep-hole to Lower Hartley Farm and a small wooden gate. Turn right up alongside the barn to another small wooden gate. Through the gate, turn left alongside the wall (L) to a similar gate. Go straight on across the path with the Orchan Rocks (R). Follow a wall (L) round and bend right up over heathland alongside the head of a valley (L), with a communications mast (L). You come to Hudson's Bridge over Redmires Water. Why is it called Hudson's Bridge?

From here walk along the Todmorden Centenary Walk with crag outcrops (L).

2.   Turn right onto Stoney Lane up across heathland to a high fence stile. Over the stile turn right down between widely spaced walls to another high fence stile. Continue to walk between deserted old farm buildings and up a paved path to another high fence stile. Go straight on through a small fence gate. Walk over an open stretch on paving slabs, some well worn, to a small fence gate.

3.   Bear down right of Whirlaw Stones. Soon, weather permitting, Stoodley Pike comes into view. After crossing a fence stile, go down past a farm with white rear wall and black window surrounds to another fence stile.

Hudson's Bridge

4. Where a lane goes down right, go straight on for 25 metres, then veer up left of a telegraph pole to squeeze between a wall (L) and a wooden gate (R). Walk on between walls and squeeze right of a wooden gate. Go on between farm buildings through double metal gates, then through the gap to the right of a metal gate — on the left is an unusual arrangement of stone water troughs under an arch. Go past the farm buildings (R), over a wall stile and alongside a wall (R). Go straight on through a gap and alongside the fence (R) to go down stone steps and over a stream. Veer up right to two fence stiles. Keep alongside the fence (L) to a fence stile at an open farm gate. After a second fence stile veer right towards a farm and a fence stile. As you pass the farm see the stone trough in the angle of the wall (L). Go out of the drive of West Hey Head Farm over a fence stile.

5. Go straight over the lane again onto the Calderdale Way past a large stone gatepost (R) with two slot holes. Go over a cattle grid, past a farmhouse and over a wall stile. Walk across the field to a fence + wall stile. Go alongside a fence (R) to two high fence stiles on either side of a sunken track with steps down and up. Continue over the crest of a stretch of heathland and down to two fence + wall stiles on either side of a track.

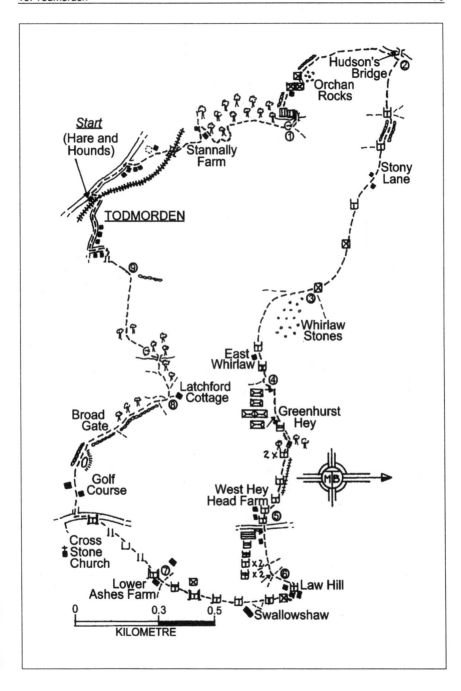

Hudson's Bridge

Orchan Rocks

Start (Hare and Hounds)

Stannally Farm

Stony Lane

TODMORDEN

Whirlaw Stones

East Whirlaw

Greenhurst Hey

Latchford Cottage

Broad Gate

Golf Course

West Hey Head Farm

Cross Stone Church

Lower Ashes Farm

Law Hill

Swallowshaw

0   0.3   0.5

KILOMETRE

6. Walk beside a fence (R), then a wall past a farm to turn right over a fence stile and down between the buildings. At the lane turn right and just inside the driveway, bear left to a fence gate, and on to a high fence stile. Go straight over the field, passing Swallowshaw (L) with its mullion windows, to a fence stile and then on to a stone pillar + fence stile. Go alongside a wall (R) past a water trough set in the wall, available to livestock on both sides. You come to a combination of a fence + stone pillar stile and small fence gate. Go straight on to a fence + wall stile, and on past Lower Ashes Farm (L) with the inscription:

+C+
A*M
1759

Go straight on round a barn to a stone pillar + fence stile. Walk alongside a wall (L) to a stone pillar stile.

There are good views over Todmorden, plus the tower of Cross Stone Church.

7. Go alongside the wall (L) to a gap at the corner of the wall. Veer left across the field to stone posts at the corner of the next field. Bend round left to a fence + stone pillar stile at the road. Turn left into the road and in 100 metres turn right onto a public bridleway (Broad Gate). Go past Durn Cottage (R) and Todmorden Golf Club (L). Go straight onto a track between walls and past a pond (R). The golf course is to the right. As the left-hand wall ends, bear up with the right-hand wall. Eventually bend round left between two well-built walls.

8. At cross-paths – Latchford Cottage (R), dated RB 1833 – go straight on uphill. In 30 metres veer left of trees and beside a fence/wall (L). Take the right-hand fork and go down to a wooden bridge over a stream. Turn left down the path to a wooden kissing gate. From hereon the path is indistinct: you need to wind around trees and bushes, undulating but not losing height, in a westerly direction; go over a tumbledown wall, and contour round between the head of a gully (L) and a pond (R).

9. Where a wall comes down from the right and ends, follow the line of the wall downhill and bear right into the bottom corner, where there is a stone pillar stile and stone steps. Turn right alongside a wall (R). Zigzag left and right and past a house (L) to a wall gap. Turn left down Ashenhurst Road. Turn right and follow the road down to go over the junction. Then zigzag right and left and under the railway bridge and down to the car park.

16: Cragg Vale

Vale Views

Distance: 8 km (5 miles)

Time: 3 hours

Map: OS Outdoor Leisure 21 (1:25 000), Landranger 104 (1:50 000)

Parking: in the vicinity of The Hinchcliffe Arms on the road from Cragg Vale up to Withens Clough Reservoir, off B6138 up from Mytholmroyd (A646)

Terrain: meadow and field, woodland, farm track, path and short stretches of road – very undulating, with some steepish ascents and descents on the first section; the terrain is moderately easy further on

Refreshments: The Hinchcliffe Arms, Cragg Vale, and in Mytholmroyd

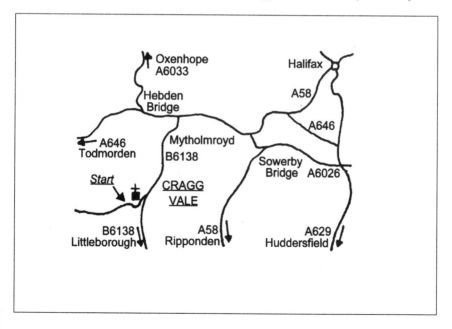

THIS most pleasant walk takes you along both sides of Cragg Vale –
often through woodland, alongside streams, and at times at a high
enough level to afford you extensive views. The colours in the au-
tumn can be exceptional.

*The Hincliffe Arms, overlooked by the Church of St John-in-the-
Wilderness, has a small display of equipment of the Cragg Coiners,
an 18th century coin-clipping and minting gang, led by 'King' David
Hartley.*

Start by walking east past The Hinchcliffe Arms (L). Turn left on the footpath at the top side of the car park and to the right of the buildings. Walk
into the trees on a terrace above the river (R). Cross a stream on boards
and continue straight on passing a tennis club (L). Go left through a wall
gap and up wooden steps, and at the top through gateposts. There is a
steep incline (R). Cross a stream on stepping stones. Go up left to
Sunny Bank Lane and out of the wood through a three-stone pillar stile.

1. Turn left up a wall (L) and right alongside a wall (L) – there is a little seat
    (R) for you to rest and look across the vale. Go up left through a wall gap
    and, past a fence and the backs of cottages (R). After going through a
    fence gate, bear left up the field and out of it at the top onto a lane. Turn
    acutely left up a road, then bend right up to Upper Lumb. Turn right
    above the barn conversion and go alongside the wall (R) to a wall stile.
    Veer up left to a fence stile.

2. Go alongside a wire fence (R), through a small metal gate and to a fence
    stile with a small wooden gate in a wall. You may now have to carve a
    path through ferns, holly bushes and trees to a fence stile. Veer down
    right to a fence stile in the corner. Turn left up between walls. 10 metres
    short of a building, cross a wall stile (R) – beware! it is steep on its far
    side. Veer left down to the end of a steep incline, and bear left uphill,
    keeping ever closer to the wood. As it levels out, find a fence stile (L) in
    mid-fence, opposite a large 'erratic' boulder. Just beyond is a small wa-
    ter channel with a stone piered exit. Cross the stile – don't go straight on
    but veer right down the field.

    *Crossing the field you get a good (and the only) view down over
    Mytholmroyd.*

3. Cross a fence stile in the bottom corner into the wood. (The path
    through the woodland is indistinct and you need to take care on the
    steep slopes.) You can follow a path round left past a prominent crag.
    As you come to the end of trees, bend round to the right and down to a

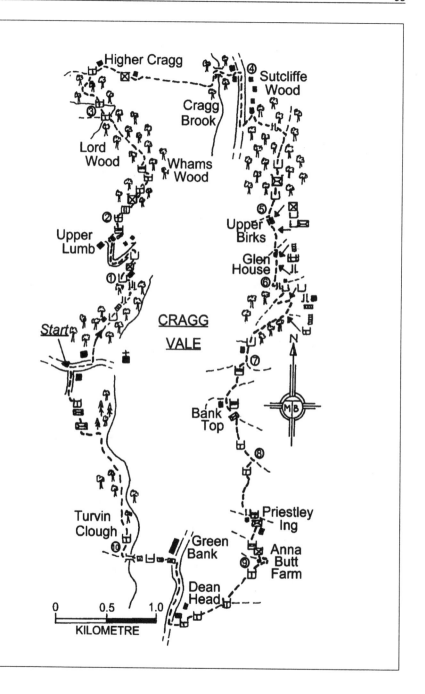

fence stile in the corner of the left bend of the fence. Turn right downhill on the track between walls topped by fences. You come out at an old farm building (Higher Cragg) – what do you notice about the way the stones were laid? Turn right down the lane between walls. Go through a small wooden gate onto a footpath (old trackway?), and across a brook. Alongside a water channel (R) veer left – do not cross stile (R) – and pass Lower Cragg Farm and go down a tarmac lane. Go left and right over Cragg Brook and up past a barn (L) dated 18WF90.

4. Turn right up the main road for 150 metres. Cross the road and go acutely left up the tarmac drive of Underwood. Turn right at the house onto a grassy track. Bend left into the trees and go straight on up, through wooden posts. Turn right alongside a fence (R), and join the path from the left. Turn right and go over brooks and boggy sections through the wood, largely of silver birch and holly. Walk eventually alongside a wall (R) and further on through a wall gap. At a post go straight on to a metal gate with very solid stone pillars. Go through a wall gap (R) and down over slabs between walls.

5. Zigzag right and left through Upper Birks. At the end of the cottages go through a small wooden gate, then a wall gap and on slabs beside a wall (R). Go through a wall gap, with metal gate (L), and bear left up the lane.

The hamlet of Upper Birks

At the house go up its left-hand side past a stone trough set in the wall (L), round and up stone steps. Go past the back of the house and through a zigzag stone stile. Veer left up a concrete and gravel track between walls and through stone gateposts, the left-hand one having slot holes.

6. At the end of the left bend, before the lane up right, turn right up stone steps and zigzag up through a wall gap. Turn right along a wall top (R) and up to cross a wall, veering leftish up to the trees (R). Follow the track left up towards a stone house standing high above a wall. Go over a track and through a wall gap, straight ahead, turning right past stone gateposts with four slots and postholes. Climb steps up left, then go right on a drive; as it bends left, go down steps and straight over a fence stile. Go alongside a wall (L) into an elongated wood over tumbledown walls until at the end emerge on the right. Go through a wall gap and on past a house (R).

Enjoy the view back and across the vale. All along the next stretch, you have extensive views over to Withens Clough Reservoir and Stoodley Pike.

7. (If you wish to shorten the walk, you can follow the Calderdale Way downhill right, which will bring you to the main road). At the left bend veer right, with a wall (L) and on to a wall stile. Over the field turn right onto a farm track and between wooden posts. Bend round left to Bank Top. The right of way goes straight on through the yard past the 17th century farm, but the 'way' is rarely dry. So the farmer prefers you to take an alternative route: just before the farm, cross a slab wall stile (L) and turn right following the fence round to cross it beside the farm gate (R) at the far end of the yard. With your back to this gate turn right and cross the field to a fence stile. Go on between a wall (L) and fence (R). On your left is a large stone gatepost with 3 large holes.

8. Bear right and follow the wire fence (R) to a fence stile. Follow the wall (L) in a left-hand sweep round to go through wooden pillars and down a stepped wall stile. Turn left up the lane for 20 metres and right through a metal gate. Go down alongside the wall (L), and at the bottom through a wall stile (or metal gate). Bear left on the bridge over a stream and through a fence gate and up to Anna Butt Farm. As requested on the sign, bear left up alongside the wall (R) and follow it round right and down to the opposite gate.

9. Bear left across the field to go over a fence stile. Follow the broken-down wall (R) across fields, aiming for a power pylon. At this turn right over a fence stile and go down alongside the wall (L) to a fence stile in the corner, with a metal gate (L). Going down a grassy track, bend left to a fence stile. Go on down the drive alongside cottages (R). Turn right down the main road for 150 metres. Just before cottages (L) at Green Bank, turn left on a footpath to Turvin Clough down stone steps. Continue downhill via wooden steps and left round a stone pillar. Take stone steps through a wall gap. Go down a flight of stone steps to a stone clapper style bridge and a little waterfall.

10. Turn right and you have alternative paths: the lower route (R) and the higher (L). Follow the path right and up against a wall (L). Go over a fence stile and veer left uphill. Opposite cottages (R) across the valley, with their roofs higher at one end than the other, there is a large stone slab with interesting markings (VI, W, a cross and other decoration). Go through stone gateposts, the right-hand one having slot holes. At a fork bear left round the corner of the wood, including fir. Then bear left onto open land and right past a metal gate and on to a fence stile on the far side of a metal gate. Exit onto a lane, signposted from Green Bank, and go down past a picturesque garden over the wall (R) at Marsh Grove.

Note the solid wall and gateway (L), leading to a former works, whose chimney is still standing, as you return to wherever you have parked your car.

17: Stoodley Pike

High Level Views

Distance: 8.8 km (5½ miles)

Time: 2½ hours

Map: OS Outdoor Leisure 21 (1:25 000), Landranger 104 (1:50 000)

Parking: at the Yorkshire Water car park below Withens Clough Reservoir, above Cragg Vale, off B6138, and up from Mytholmroyd (A646)

Terrain: after an initial ascent the terrain is mostly open moorland paths and farm tracks, though there are some wet stretches on the way back

Refreshments: The Hinchcliffe Arms, Cragg Vale, and in Mytholmroyd

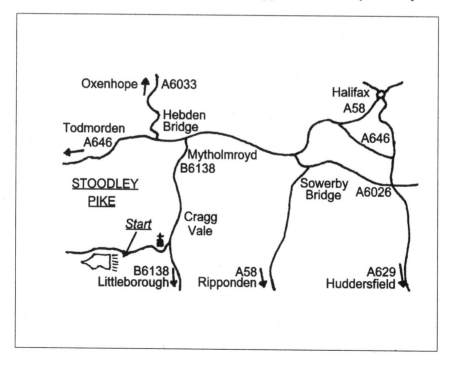

Stoodley Pike

THIS is a most pleasant walk for a fine weather day. It is also surprisingly easy walking after an initial ascent up onto the ridge where the Pennine Way goes past the outstanding landmark of Stoodley Pike. You cannot fail to gaze at the extensive views over northern Calderdale, and further on over Cragg Vale. **Note:** take a compass with you.

Starting from the car park walk westwards, signposted to Withens New Road and Mankinholes, through the wooden gate up to Withens Clough Reservoir. As you level out alongside the reservoir and pass The Pastures (R), you can see Stoodley Pike peeping over the horizon. On the left bend ignore (R) the path and further on Calderdale Way. Follow the bends to left and right.

1.   At the end of the wall (R) bear up the right-hand track heading for a deserted building (Red Dykes). At the left bend, go straight up the grassy way-marked path. Go on uphill past several lone gateposts until you come to a wall (L). Further up, the Calderdale Way joins from the right and a double-walled lane goes off left to Red Dykes. Go straight on up through impressive stone gateposts, with solid bases, and squeeze pillars (R). Follow a wall (L) up to the wooden Withens Gate. Just before it is a stone pillar inscribed with a cross and TE DEUM LAUDAMUS – what used to happen at this pillar? Through the gate walk straight on over a slabbed pavement until you come to cross-paths on the edge of the ridge.

Turning right, all along the ridge you get extensive views over to various tors, Todmorden, Lobb Mill, a couple of windfarms, Hebden Bridge and beyond.

2.   Walking on the Pennine Way you reach Stoodley Pike Monument:

A PEACE MONUMENT
Erected by Public Subscription
Commenced in 1814 to commemorate the surrender of
Paris
Finished after the battle of Waterloo in 1815.
The Pike fell on the day after the Russian Ambassador
left London before the declaration of war with Russia.
Rebuilt when peace was restored 1856.

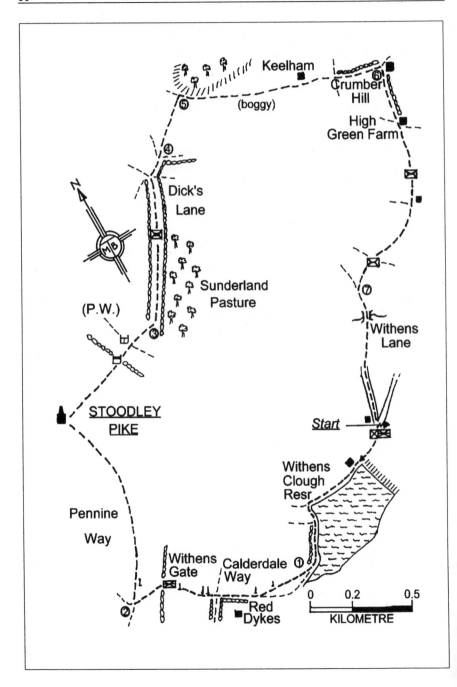

After gazing your fill, turn eastwards down the hillside to a wall stile. Pass a fence stile (L), leading on to the Pennine Way, and carry on alongside a wall (L).

3. Bear left onto Dick's Lane between widely spaced walls. Halfway along, go through a metal gate. At cross-paths continue straight on, signposted to Daisy Bank.

4. When the wall (R) turns right, the path becomes indistinct: the right of way goes in a north east direction, until you turn right onto a path; but it is suggested that you go straight on across open country in an ENE direction — aim slightly left of the nearest farm building, until you come to the edge of a wooded valley.

5. Turn right and skirt the valley (L) over well worn slabs here and there. Take care: there are boggy sections with potholes, but a couple of way-marked posts help. After more slabs bear right onto a farm track. Pass a farm (L) and follow the wall (L) for a distance to the next farm, Crumber Hill.

6. At the junction, turn right alongside a wall (L) and then up between walls past High Green Farm with an ornate brass post box (L). Go along a farm track and through a metal gate. The track bends up round right to another metal gate. Continue between walls.

7. At a junction bear left down a tarmac lane through trees, crossing a stream with waterfall (R). Carry on down the lane to the car park.

18: Hebden Dale

The Three Valleys Walk

Distance: (A) 12 km (7½ miles); (B) 9.6 km (6 miles); (C) 7 km (4½ miles)

Map: OS Outdoor Leisure 21, Landranger 104 (1:50 000)

Time: (A) 4 hours; (B) 3 hours; (C) 2½ hours

Parking: in the National Trust car park or its overflow park above New Bridge on Midgehole Lane left off A6033, north of Hebden Bridge, grid reference: 988293

Terrain: path, track, woodland and moorland, field and short stretches of undulating road with a number of steepish ascents and descents

Refreshments: many in Hebden Bridge; also, at The Cross Inn or White Horse in Heptonstall

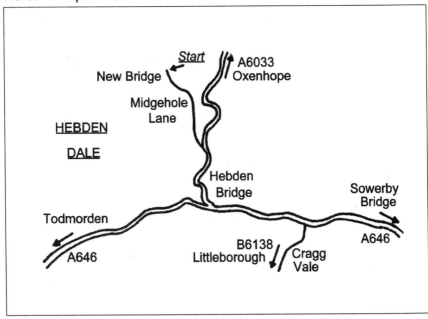

ALL the walks have level and strenuous parts, but they are full of delightful scenery and special points of interest. They lead you through wooded deans/dales, typical of this part of Calderdale. Walks A and B also take you high up over an open moorland between two 'deans', past famous crags and a former mill. Walks A and C take you through the picturesque and much visited hamlet of Heptonstall.

Walk A and B: Turning right out of the car park, go up round the right-hand bend with Hollin Hall Wood (L) and Green Hurst Wood (R). Walk up the road past the YWA (1951) pumping station (L) and the National Trust office (R). Go onto a gravel track through woodland. At a junction (L), with a seat in memory of Lewis Fitton Tordoff, carry straight on. In 100 metres there is another seat set back (L), dedicated to Dent Sutcliffe. Go across a stretch of open ground (R).

1. As you enter woodland, bear right down alongside a wall (R). After 25 metres, ignore the leftward path and continue following the wall downhill to meet a level track coming in from the right (where a field gate can be seen set in the wall). Turn left along this track. Note the dam in the valley bottom below and the cultivated trees across the stream (R). Go on down right and alongside the stream to a stone packhorse bridge (R). Turn right over it and veer left up a flagged path under overhanging trees alongside a wall (R). At the top turn left round a house and go steeply up the tarmac road past 2 huge millstone gateposts leading to a cottage.

2. Up at the road bend, bear left and on stones over a stream. Go up round a holly bush (L) alongside a fence (L) through trees. Go over a wall + fence stile, beside a wall (L) and up past a post (R). Cross the field diagonally until you come to a wall. Turn right up alongside this wall (L) all the way up to a wall stile (L) at the top of the field. Go left over this stile and follow the wall (R) to a wall stile beside stone gateposts (L). Continue on a flagged path and over a drainage channel past farm buildings (R). Go over a wall stile with a gatepost base and past a farm (L) with a tractor weather vane. Cross a spring (R) to a fence + wall stile (L). Turn right into a lane for 10 metres. Go through a small wooden gate ahead in the wall. Bear diagonally right to a fence stile, with a metal gate (R). Walk on the right-hand side of a farm through a small fence gate, then a wall gap and past a barn/shed (L) and onto Haworth Old Road. In 100 metres veer left down a bridleway (Lumb Lane) and turn left down between a fence (L) and wall (R). Eventually you are walking down cobbles, with noticeable grooves. Note also the stone cut into thin layers below the semi-circular toppers in the wall (R).

3. Bear right with the wall to view a waterfall. Cross a stream on slabs and turn left across the hump-back Lumb Bridge over Crimsworth Dean Beck. Go left up the slabbed trackway, viewing the beck tumbling over lichen and fern covered slabs into a deep pool. Going up between walls you pass 2 stone gateposts with posthole slots (L). You gain a good view of Stoodley Pike (L) as you go up past a small stone trough (R) and derelict buildings (L). Bear left at the first and up between walls onto the Haworth to Hebden Bridge Walk – the South Pennine Packhorse Trail. At the junction of tracks, turn acutely right towards Grain Water Bridge. Go straight on at Nook: the building has an old fire range, fireplaces and stone staircases. Go past a stone trough (L).

4. As the path levels out before Hardibut Clough, veer up left through a wall and bend round left to head for a ladder stile in mid-wall – the path is indistinct through rushes. Over the stile turn left alongside a wall, distorting with age.

   Over the wall (L) is Coddy, a derelict farmhouse of different types of construction, dressed and dry stone, and with a circular window on its end. Further on round, look across the field (L) and you can see a wall with a row of regular square holes built into it – why was it so built?

5. Bend round right with the wall (L). Eventually a reservoir will come into view. Go through a small wooden gate (L) and follow the wall (R) round to the left. Continue round to a wooden farm gate. Go on over a stream and on past a wooden post at the end of a wall (R). Cross fields to go between walls. Note the wall (L) round the field built with stones sticking out. At a bend is a now blocked sheephole. Go through a wooden farm gate and straight on into the Walshaw farm complex. At the junction, go left down between buildings to a wall stile (L). Over it, turn right alongside the wall (R). Go through a wooden farm gate and straight down past an old galvanised lamppost with a rifle weather vane.

   Look back at the façade of the main house, which has a view down several valleys and across to Stoodley Pike.

6. Go down the field and through a small wooden gate in the wall. Enter a mixed woodland, including fir, oak and birch. Go down stone steps to zigzag left and right (as the bridge ahead is closed). Below more steps there is a waterfall (L). Carry on downhill until going through wooden posts turn left onto a track and over a stream. Continue straight on uphill

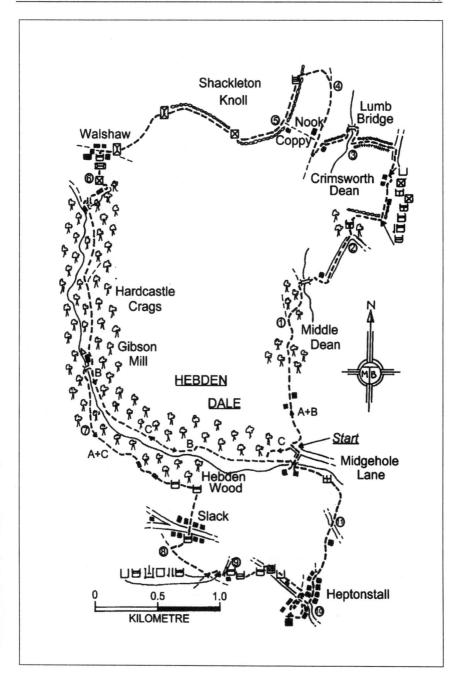

Shackleton
Knoll

Lumb
Bridge

Walshaw

⑤ Nook
Coppy

④

③

Crimsworth
Dean

⑥

Hardcastle
Crags

Gibson
Mill

B

HEBDEN

DALE

① Middle
Dean

N

M B

A+B

⑦

B

A+C

C

C

Start

Midgehole
Lane

②

Hebden
Wood

Slack

⑧

⑨

⑪

Heptonstall

⑩

0   0.5   1.0

KILOMETRE

and to a seat (R). Join a main track from the left and go steadily downhill past the famous Hardcastle Crags and a log cabin shelter. Just below on your right is a weir and straight on a mill.

Gibson Mill, built in 1801 as a water powered cotton mill, was rebuilt in 1860; its 5 hp. water-fed wheel was found to be inadequate and changed to a steam boiler with a chimney. Beyond the mill is a 'private' road over the bridge with toll charges in old 'd' pence still displayed.

Walk A and C: Cross the river either by the toll bridge, or slightly lower down by stepping stones (R). Turn left and up a track alongside a wall (L), past a shelter (R) and on over cobbles. At a junction of paths go straight on and ignore the stone steps (R). Go on uphill over several brooks to a 'clearing' in the trees. Go straight over onto a path which goes steeply uphill, including stone steps. As it levels out, note the large block foundations of the wall (R).

7.   At a fork, bear right up stone steps and alongside a wire fence (R). Go round a wall end (R) and a holly bush (L) to a wall stile. Cross the field alongside a wall (L) to a wall stile. Turn right up a broad track between walls and at the top pass November Cottage (R). Cross the road at Slack. Walk over the front garden (!) and down the side of Poppyfields House (L). At a fence gate ahead turn right over a wall stile, and left down a ginnel following the wall (L) round right. At the wall end, go straight on past the gardens of houses (R).

8.   Turn left onto a gravel track. At cross-paths, overlooking Colden Clough below, turn left through a wall gap with a large stone beyond, inscribed with JT2 (?). Walk on between a wire fence (L) and a low wall (R). Go over a wall stile, then a wall stile + small fence gate. Walk over slabs to a small wooden gate past Fields Farm (R). Go through a wall + pillar stile and along to a small fence gate. Over a metal gate (L) is a water trough. Carry on alongside a wall (L), through a concrete pillar stile and over a wall stile.

9.   Go straight over a lane to a wall stile (L) and alongside a wall (R) to a wall stile. Fork left over slabs across the field. Go through a wall stile with the bottom stone well worn. Turn right for 20 metres and cross over the road, veering left up to a wall gap + small wooden gate. Cross the field on slabs and go through a wall gap. Continue down between a fence (L) and wall (R), over which is the local school. At the bottom go through a wall gap opposite Whitehall Fold, and turn right into Townfield Lane.

Gibson Mill pond and artwork

You are now in the picturesque hamlet of Heptonstall. Take your time to wander around: opposite is Weavers Square; ahead is Church Street along which is the site of the Cockpit, in use during the Napoleonic Wars; round the corner is the 'new' church of St Thomas a Beckett and St Thomas the Apostle; in the middle are the remains of the earlier church, originally AD1260; in Churchyard Bottom is the former Grammar School, now the Museum; and beyond a stone archway, is the Cloth Hall, c.1545-58.

10. Turn right for a few metres, with the White Lion and The Cross Inn (L). Turn left into Northgate. See the house (L) with the inscription 17HE36 above a carved tableau depicting a man wearing a cocked hat and sword and a lady with a fan, both with hands on a tree – what tree? Further on is an archway (L) inscribed TB 1578. Ignore the path (R), though down it is an interesting octagonal Wesleyan Chapel. Beyond, take the right fork past Stocks Villas (L). Wind down past cottages and the driveway of North Well House (R).

11. Cross the road and go on down the path ahead. Cross a lane and continue down cobbles. Once on the level go through zigzag fences beside 2 small weirs. Past the houses (L) cross right over the bridge and up the lane. Turn left onto the road and return to wherever you have parked your car.

Walk B is a shortened form of **Walk A**, cutting out the ascent over to Heptonstall, and taking you straight back down Hebden Dale to the car:

Leaving Gibson Mill, carry on past stepping stones on the left-hand bank of the river. At another set of stepping-stones veer left uphill on the red route which soon returns you down to the river bank. At a third set of stepping stones, go left up stone stones, then right along a terrace with stone edgings. Continue on a paved/cobbled path past a weir and seat (R). Wind your way around and on past yet another weir. Stone steps lead you back up on to the main track. Continue until you come to the end of the path beside a bridge. Turn left up the lane and again left onto the road to return to your car.

Walk C takes you up through Hebden Dale to Gibson Mill and then joins **Walk A** to go up and over to Heptonstall:

Turn right out of the car park and almost immediately take a path to the left into the woodland. When you come to a clearing you drop down left to turn right onto a main track. From thereon you wind your way around and over (in parts) a cobbled/paved track. Eventually the track bends left downhill to stepping stones across the river. Continue on the right-hand bank past another set of stepping-stones. Reaching Gibson Mill, join **Walk A** by turning left over the toll bridge.

19: Luddenden Dean

A Typical Dean

Distance: 7 km (4½ miles)

Map: OS Outdoor Leisure 21 (1:25 000), Landranger 104 (1:50 000)

Time: 2½ hours

Parking: in Luddenden Dean off A646, in a public car park at Jerusalem Farm and Education Centre on Jerusalem Lane, grid reference: 038278

Terrain: path, track, woodland, field and short stretches of road, undulating with a couple of moderately steep ascents

Refreshments: at Cat-i-th-Well Inn at Caty Well Bridge (restricted opening hours); several in Sowerby Bridge

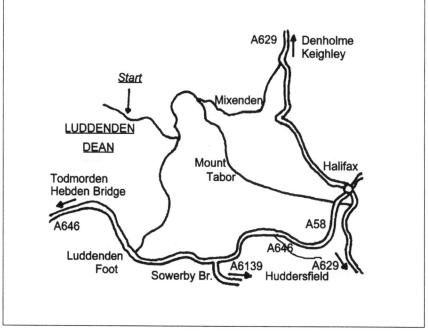

The Lowe Farm

THIS walk takes you through delightful parts of a typical Calderdale
dean as well as affording you extensive views at high level on both
sides of the dean.

Starting from Jerusalem Farm go down to the bottom of the car park and
through a V-shaped fence stile. Continue alongside a wall (L) on a terrace down into the dean. Cross the cobbled Wade Bridge and walk on
up alongside the stream (L) to a fence stile. Follow the high path straight
on until you have to zigzag down left to a wooden footbridge + gate.
Bear diagonally left up the field to a fence stile, then up beside a brook
(R) and over a wall to a fence stile. Go on uphill to a wooden gate. Pass
a telegraph post to a fence stile and go up alongside a wire fence (L).
Across (R) is the impressive Upper Mytholm Barn. Cross a terraced
bridge, left up a driveway and turn right onto a track between walls.

1.   Walk on and round through a cutting with large vertically placed slabs
      (R). In the field (L) note how the wall has been constructed with horizon-
      tal courses up the hillside. Across the valley is a small cemetery with,
      further up on the ridge, a house with castellations. Continue on Wood
      Lane and opposite Catherine House there is a little stone trough set in
      the wall (L), just before the junction with many metal gates. Go through
      two metal gates.

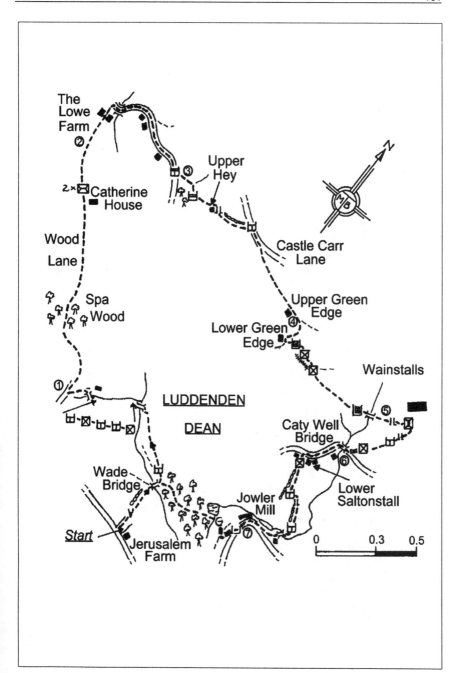

2.   Walk on until you descend to The Lowe Farm with its ornate archway and mock castellations on the buildings on either side of the lane. There is no right of way ahead to the reservoirs, so turn acutely right down a cobbled road, over Luddenden Brook and up between walls. Halfway up (R) see over the wall the huge bole of a tree set in the wall. Ignoring the footpath (L), go up past Lowe Cottage (R), the ornate gateposts of The Lowe, and some large 'erratic' rocks in the field (L). Just past a house (R) and 30 metres over the brow of the road, climb stone steps up left through a wall + fence stile.

3.   Bear diagonally across the field to the top right-hand corner alongside a wall (R), beside the wood. Go up over a stream and a tumbledown wall to follow a wall (R) to a wall stile in the corner. Veer diagonally left up the field towards a derelict barn (Upper Heys). Go left of it, over a tumble-down wall, between stone gateposts and round and up alongside the wall (L). Near the top pass a spring (R) and two old wooden railway wagons, and reach a fence stile in a wall. Turn right onto the lane and in 100 metres veer right onto a part gravel, part tarmac track.

You gain a fine view down the dean.

4.   Just past Upper Green Edge Farm (R) take the right fork, round a right-hand bend and down the track. Zigzag left, right and left until opposite a farm and past a wall (L), go up left to a wall stile + small wooden gate. Follow a wall (R) up through rushes and a slightly boggy stretch and through a small fence gate. Follow the wire fence (R) and zigzag left and right to a fence gate. The path ahead is indistinct: veer left for a renovated mill in the distance; cross a channel and some streams; go through a small fence gate + wall stile; cross a well-channelled stream on large double slabs. Go on between stone gateposts, though the wall is now non-existent and go round a wall (L).

There is a converted mill ahead. See the overflow down the wall from the mill dam above. Shortly you go down a wooded glen with a waterfall down right.

5.   Go through a metal gate and turn right along a gravel track and follow a wall (R) through wooden posts, with a metal gate (L). Go down between walls past stone steps (L) and through a fence onto a grassy track downhill with a wall (L). At the bottom of the path go through a small fence gate and down vertical stone slab steps with a metal railing (R).

On the top side of Caty Well Bridge, see the waterfall cascading through a stone arch tunnel and under a metal water channel, now filled in. On the bottom side is the charmingly named Cat-i-th-Well

Inn, with a stone trough set in the wall opposite, but where is the 'Well'?

Caty Well bridge

6. Turn right over the bridge and bend round past the Inn. After a right bend and entering the derestricted speed area, turn left after the first house at Lower Saltonstall down a lane between cottages to a fence gate. Follow the well-built wall (R) down. At a fence stile, bear left over the field to two stone pillars, the left with postholes. Turn right down alongside a wall (R) to a fence stile. Go down right to a bridge with a waterfall (L) onto a road. Go alongside a pond (R) and up left of four-storey cottages, (2 up and 2 down). Carry on down a cobbled and concrete road.

7. In 80 metres go through a wall gap (R) and down steep stone and wooden steps. Go left onto a track for a few metres and turn right down more wooden steps to a wooden kissing gate and cross the dam wall. The dam is set in a most picturesque glen. Walk straight on, winding your way through trees over cobbles. At the fork go left downhill, with the stream tumbling down (L), to cross the bridge. Bear left back up to Jerusalem Farm.

20: Rishworth

Reservoirs and Mill Ponds

Distance: 8.8 km (5½ miles)

Time: 2½ hours

Map: OS Outdoor Leisure 21 (1:25 000), Landranger 110 (1:50 000)

Parking: in the public car park at Ryburn Reservoir, south off A58 (Rochdale Road), approx. 2 km from the centre of Ripponden; left down Swift Place, 70 metres beyond the derestricted sign, grid reference: 024187

Terrain: meadow and field, woodland and moorland, farm track and path, short stretches of road – undulating with short steepish ascents and descents

Refreshments: several in Rishworth and Ripponden

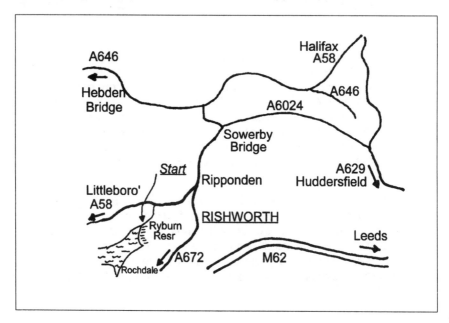

THIS is quite a strenuous but varied walk with lots of interest. It starts with circling Ryburn Reservoir, passing 17th century farm-houses before taking you up high enough to overlook M62. It goes down a former trackway, then alongside woodland across the valley from Rishworth School, before returning you up a wooded glen.

Upper Cockcroft Farm, near Rishworth

You may be lucky enough to see herons, as the Ryburn Reservoir is one of their haunts.

Starting from the car park with the reservoir (L) and facing west, cross a fence stile slightly right and go straight on along the permissive path across the field to a fence stile. Enter the wood, mainly of fir. Go on beyond a wall end (R), across streamlets. Further on go down wooden steps, over a bridge alongside a metal pipe, up steps and on through the wood. Carry on occasionally over streamlets, slabs, tumbledown walls and past crags (L). Go left over the wooden bridge, signposted 'Back o' th' Height'. Note the iron oxide in the stream.

1.   Turn right up steps to the wall, then left up stone steps to a fence stile. Continue up, alongside a wall (R), and up stone steps to a wall stile. More steps take you through posts. At a signpost turn left and right

around ruined buildings and up to a small wooden gate. There is a good view back across the valley. Follow the path towards Lower Wormald. Follow the wall (L) to a wall gap; go through and over a fence stile veering diagonally right for farm buildings. Go through a wall stile + wooden kissing gate. Go diagonally on over slabs to a wooden kissing gate + stone pillar stile. Walk between narrow walls and bend right to go between buildings. Turn right and immediately left over a wall + fence stile to Ryburn Reservoir.

2. Follow the wall (R) down to a fence stile in the bottom corner. Go diagonally right through a copse of firs to a fence stile. Follow the fence (R) down to cross it via a fence stile (R). Continue down stone steps to cross a fence stile and a wooden bridge over Hutch Brook, as it cascades down a mini-gorge. Go up wooden steps and left under trees. At the end turn right and follow the fence (R) bearing up left. At the top go over a fence stile.

There are interesting features on farms ahead: on Cockcroft Farm, note LEH 1649 (indistinct) over the main door (L), and BSH 1709 over the window (opposite); on Upper Cockcroft Farm, a dovecote over the main door.

3. Turn left onto a track and through a metal farm gate. Walk up a stony track between walls. Go over a fence stile and past houses. Turn acutely right in front of Cockcroft Farm. Having passed the farm and a stone trough (R), turn left up alongside Bowler's Cottage (L), not on the farm track. Turn left to a wall gap + fence stile. Bear diagonally left along the line of the poles. Note the stone slabs standing on end (R) – part of the field boundary. Go through a small wooden gate and on between walls.

4. Turn left in front of Upper Cockcroft Farm (L), and follow the stream (R) to cross it over slabs; what is interesting about the construction of the wall (L)? Go over a fence stile and follow the line of poles to another fence stile. Turn left down the road. At the next left bend cross the fence stile (R). Bear diagonally left through the fence and to a fence stile. Keep going diagonally over the playing field to the bottom right-hand corner. At the wall turn right. Do NOT turn left through the stonehenge-type gateway + small wooden gate, but go straight on through a metal gate. Take care: the way ahead may be very boggy; bear slightly right on the left of a pylon to a small wooden kissing gate.

5. Go straight on between a fence (L) and wall (R) to a wooden kissing gate. Continue through a metal gate past a barn (L). Before the house,

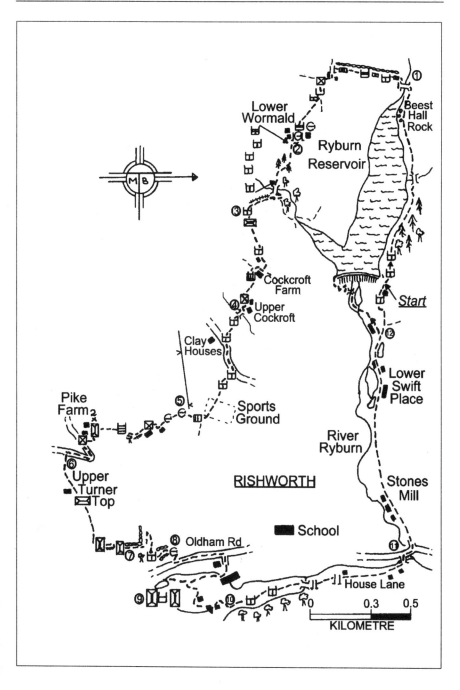

bear right up a fence (L) to a small wooden gate. Go left alongside the fence (L). Towards its end, veer right of a tree over slabs to a ladder stile. Bear diagonally right aiming for a farm and barn. At the top of the field go through two metal gates at Pike Farm. Go left and up round right on a farm track to a small wooden gate. Turn left onto the road following it round bends. Go over the bridge at Pike Clough (R), then bend right and up a steep hill.

6. At the top turn left on a farm track. You get a fine view of the Ryburn valley (L) and a glimpse of M62 ahead. At a fork, bear left and down past Upper Turner Top. Go through a metal gate, the right gatepost has postholes. Continue downhill, and at the right-hand bend, turn left through a metal gate and follow the wall (R). In 70 metres turn right through a metal gate.

7. Turn left to walk down the field alongside the wall. At the wall corner (L), the right of way goes straight down to turn left at the wall; but it is suggested that you go straight on down for 15 metres, then turn left on a grassy path and bend acutely right down through rushes to a fence stile with stone steps (a former mounting block?) on its far side. Go on down a former trackway between walls; note the left-hand wall – why was it built so solidly? and at the bottom it is built round an old oak tree – well polished by scratching sheep?

8. Go through a wooden kissing gate. Turn right into Godly Lane, then left into Oldham Road. Cross the road and in 250 metres turn right into Rishworth Mill Lane. Follow the road past Rishworth (Heathfield) School buildings (R) and on round right past a former (converted) mill. At an acute left bend, go straight on to view the mill race, sluice gate and pond.

9. Retrace your steps to the bend and bear right uphill past Rishworth Mill and Farm (L) with two sets of impressive stone gateposts: look back to see a dovecote on the barn end; also opposite is a metal gate – into a private wood? Beyond the wood (R) as the road bends right, go straight on through a metal gate and down between walls to a metal bar stile. Note the stone water trough (R) and the barn end with its small panes. Left round the barn go through a metal gate with dressed stone gateposts. Turn left alongside a fence (L) past an oak tree to a fence stile in the bottom left-hand corner, with a babbling stream ahead.

10. You may also espy herons on this stretch. Turn left over the stile and walk along the edge of a wood (R). Go over a fence stile and further on into the trees to a footbridge and through gateposts. Go up the slope to a wooden pillar stile through the wall, and on past a house (L) with doveholes on its far end. Take the left fork downhill on a stony track. You get sight of the main Rishworth School (L). Down at the bottom turn left over the bridge and up Holme House Lane.

11. Cross the main road. Bear right and left up a lane on a bridleway. In 110 metres high up (R) is the stone entrance to a tunnel. Just beyond, by metal railings is a thin tapering building with an ornamental cornice. Go on past Lower Stones (R), Ryburn and Whiteley Terraces, Brook Trout Cottage (L) and Lower Swift Place with a decaying watering hole in a wall arch opposite. Continue past a sluice gate (R) with over the wall a mill race + tunnel.

12. Further on at a former paper mill site, take the left fork past dilapidated buildings and alongside the river (L). Go on past the run-off from the mill pond (R), then left over the reservoir outflow. Turn right and zigzag your way up the slope, including over stone steps. Emerge at the top to turn right over the dam wall of the reservoir, and back to your car.

The reservoir has mock castellations, and you get a magnificent view left up to Baitings Reservoir.

21: Calder and Hebble

The Towpath and Topping Stones Walk

Distance: 9 km (5¾ miles)

Time: 2½ hours

Map: OS Explorer 288 (1:25 000), Landranger 104 (1:50 000)

Parking: in the car park, south of A6025 between Elland and Brighouse, below Cromwell House, close to the Calder and Hebble Canal, grid reference: 124225

Terrain: canal towpath, meadow and field, farm track, path, woodland and short stretches of road – a mixture of level walking and some steepish uphill pulls and moderate downhill stretches

Refreshments: on A6025 the Colliers Arms between Park Nook Lock and Elland Lock or at the Barge and Barrel at the Elland end of A6025

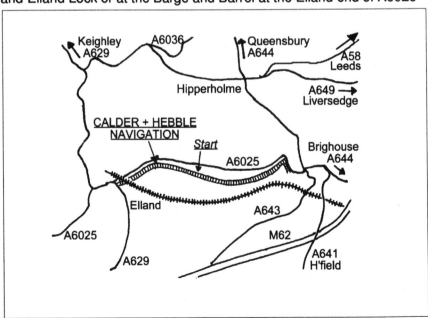

Bridge on the Calder and Hebble Canal

THIS is a walk of contrasts. It starts and finishes on the towpath of the Calder and Hebble Canal; in between it climbs high up through attractive oak woodland and close to Southowram before descending through a further two equally picturesque mixed woods. A special feature of this walk is the huge wall topping stones alongside former trackways.

Start southwards out of the parking place over a concrete bridge with metal railings. Turn left and down two flights of stone steps and left onto the towpath to go under the stone bridge with red brick parapets. Continue through metal gates. Bend left and, after more metal gates, go up past Park Nook Lock. On your right is the Colliers Arms. At Elland Lock cross over the canal and go down over the overflow to walk on along Park Road. You go past the milestone to Elland (L). Just before the restricted 30 mph sign, turn right up Plains Lane.

1.   Veer right and up in front of a row of stone houses (L). At the end go straight ahead onto a track made of red brick core between overgrown walls. You continue more steeply uphill onto a concrete, then again red brick track, into the woodland.

2. About 70 metres beyond a holly bush and wall, turn right on a well de-
    fined path. Go past a small wall on the path beside a holly bush. Take
    the left fork bearing uphill – (downhill right are gateposts with sliding
    slots for posts) – until it levels out. Wind round and through the oak
    trees, over a brook and past a pond (L), and then bear left uphill past
    gateposts (L). Go round trees (R), down and up steps over a wet/muddy
    patch, to go up the left track between walls.

    *This must have been an important former trackway judging by the
    huge topping stones to the walls. On the right are gateposts with a
    mason's mark.*

3. Continue uphill increasingly steeply, ignoring a left fork, until you take a
    left bend. Then bend right and left again onto a level stretch – note the
    double row of topping stones holding back the bank (L). Go onto an
    open track past a pylon (L) and on between walls. There is a view
    across open country (R). Go straight ahead, past Southowram Cricket
    Club (R) and through a wooden kissing gate. Ignore the 'no through
    road' (R) and carry straight on up the road past a wall of huge slab
    blocks (L). On your right is a former school with an inscription: THIS
    SCHOOL ws (sic) BUILT by subscriptions for children of all Denomi-na-
    tions AD MDCCCXXV.

4. Immediately turn right down School Lane onto the Calderdale Way. At
    the bottom go over a wooden bar stile between Jerusalem Square (L)
    and End Cottage Stables (R) into a ginnel. Pass a horse exercise
    ground and continue onto a grassy track beside a high wall (L). Zigzag
    right and left with a hedge (L) and go through a stone pillar stile. Go
    down the field to a wall gap in the bottom left corner. Turn right on a farm
    track for 20 metres. Take an acute left turn down beside a high wall (L)
    to squeeze between it and a stone pillar. Bend right over cobble setts
    and a stream and uphill between walls.

    *The next stretch takes you down Cromwell Wood with a most
    attractive valley (R). Beyond the wood there is a view across to
    Elland (R) and to Brighouse (L).*

5. At the cross-paths turn right for Cromwell Bottom between walls and
    into a wood. Continue down through mixed woodland until you eventu-
    ally exit from it. Just before the end of the track, follow stone steps left up
    to a small metal gate. Go up between narrow walls over many slabs to
    another small metal gate and zigzag slab stile. Carry on steeply over
    more slabs to a solid (sawn-off telegraph pole) fence stile.

6. Veer right on a track between walls into Freemason's Wood. Follow the

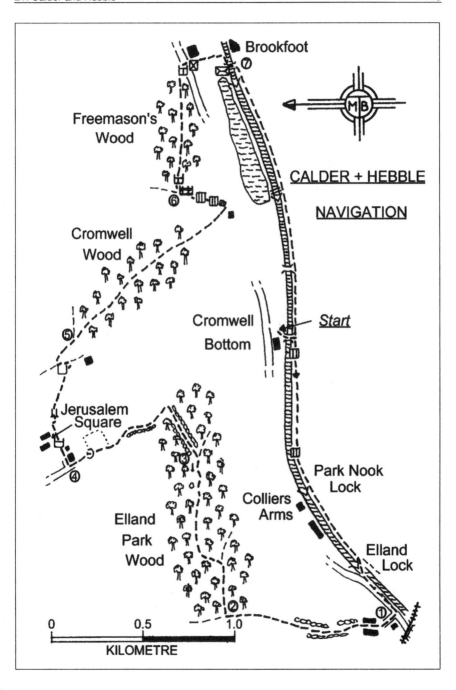

path as it levels out and then drops down towards the road (ignoring a path forking steeply down right), and go over a fence stile. Cross the road, go through a fence gate and continue to the canal bank. Turn right and go past a metal gate to turn left over the canal bridge at Brookfoot Lock.

7.   Turn right and walk along the towpath until you reach the original bridge, where you go up steps to the left and turn right over the bridge to your car.

Note at Cromwell Lock the Leeds Steel Builders 1895 bridge. Just before the last bridge on the walk, beside a seat is a stone milestone with the inscription 'From FALL ING 17 miles' – why Fall Ing and where is it?

22: Greetland

Both sides of Norland Moor

Distance: 13.3 km (8¼ miles)

Time: 4 hours

Map: OS Outdoor Leisure 21 (1:25 000), Landranger 104 (1:50 000)

Parking: in the Rochdale Road car park at Brow Bridge, West Vale, in the angle of two roads, B6112 and B6113, grid reference: 097213

Terrain: meadow, field, woodland and open moorland, path, farm track and stretches of road – undulating in the first and final sections sandwiching lengthy and moderate ascents up and around Norland Moor

Refreshments: in Norland Town or several in Greetland

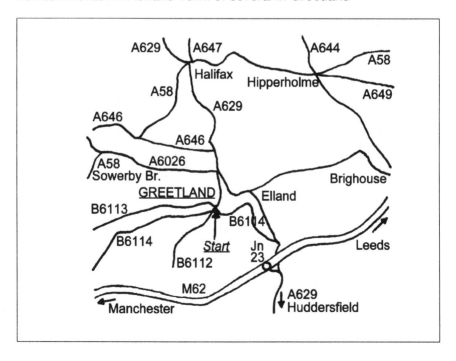

THIS walk, the longest in the Calderdale section of this book, has great variety in terrain and interest. It starts in the centre of Greetland, therefore, you have to walk along some streets and past some works before enjoying a lengthy stretch alongside a stream through fields and past former mills. A steady ascent takes you up high onto Norland Moor. You descend into the Calder valley through woodland and down an ancient trackway. You again ascend into Norland Town via a well and some superb examples of 17th century architecture. Your return is up through a wood to a ridge with extensive views across the valley to Sowerby Bridge and Halifax before you descend eventually past Clay House.

Exiting from the car park into Rochdale Road, veer left over into a cobbled street (signposted 'No Entry'). Go straight over the main road into Green Lane. Cross another main road, still on Green Lane, uphill and past the former Middle Dean Street Chapel AD1865 (R). Further on is an imposing 'period' building, dated 1907 (R). Take the right-hand fork downhill and again cross the main road, into Little Bradley. Go onto a track over a stream (R). Walk alongside the stream (R) over large slabs to a concrete bridge with metal railings.

As you walk up the valley alongside the stream with its several weirs, you may be lucky enough to see herons.

1.   Crossing the bridge, turn left through a pillar stile and walk beside the stream (L). At the field end go through a wall stile with a stone pillar. Go on past a car park and works (R). At a fork veer right – do not cross the river – and follow the rail guard (L) round. Alongside the last shed (R) veer left down onto a riverside path through trees. Emerge out through the wall and concrete poles. Go on over the field to a fence stile and past a large stone pillar with pole slots. Go over the lane and down stone steps, and squeeze through the wall past a wooden pillar (L).

2.   Continue alongside the river and through what once was a metal kissing gate, and then on to a fence stile. Go through a small fence gate and over stones towards mills in the distance. Cross streams on wooden slats and stones. There is a weir (L). At the end of the field, pass through a wooden kissing gate. Keep to the right of the first building, then walk between the further buildings of Bowers Mill. As the lane turns up right, zigzag down left and right alongside the mill dam. Near its end, turn up right, following the fence round to the stone steps. At the road, turn right for 40 metres.

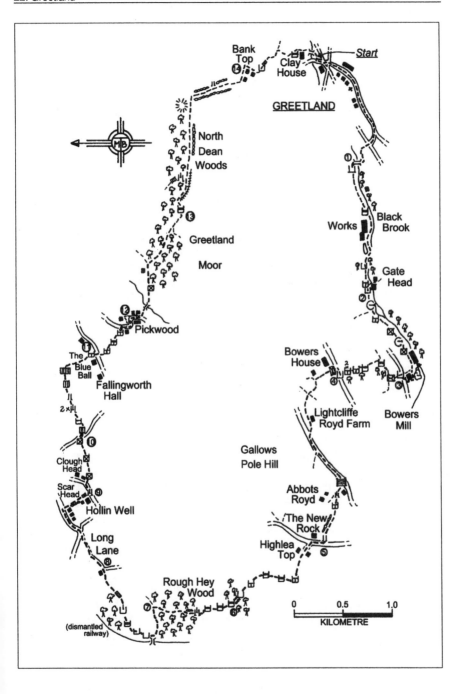

3.   Cross the road and go through a wall gap with pillar. Walk up the field beside a wall (R) and through a wall gap with a pillar to the right of a metal gate. Go through stone gateposts and veer right up through the trees to a wall stile, with a metal gate (R). Turn right through beech trees up to a wall stile. Turn left up the field alongside a wall with some trees (L) to a stone pillar stile, then a fence stile and eventually up between walls. You come to two fence stiles and go through a wall gap onto Saddleworth road (B6114). Turn right for 60 metres. Turn left up the public bridleway before Bowers House.

Bowers House has a big blue clock on its wall and a mallard duck weather vane atop horses' heads. As you go up onto Greetland Road, enjoy the view across the valley and as far as M62.

4.   Go through a metal gate and stone gateposts, and up between walls. As the lane bends right, veer up left in front of a barn and follow the wall round right. Cross the minor road onto a public bridleway, up between walls and past Lightcliffe Royd Farm (L). At Greetland Road (B6113) bear left and walk for some 450 metres. Entering a 30mph area, turn right at a bus stop (R) onto a drive over a cattle grid between gateposts. Shortly, by a power pole, veer left through a three-pillar stone stile and across the field to a fence stile, passing a 'water feature' (R) – what is it? Walk up alongside a wall (R), through an open gateway and through a squeeze stone pillar stile.

5.   At the road turn right past The New Rock and Restaurant. In 50 metres turn left on the Calderdale Way – there is a stone-built platform (L) for milk churns. Go past Highlea Top (R) and down the lane between walls. Just below a left bend, turn right over a wall + fence stile and go on to a wall stile. Go down the field to a wall stile, then keeping the holly trees on your left, continue to a fence stile. Cross stone slabs over a stream and pass up through a wall into a narrow, wooded valley. Cross another small stream and immediately fork left downhill. After 25 metres, at a junction, again take the lower left-hand path. Cross several streamlets. At the next junction, take the right-hand path, with a low wall (L).

6.   Go over a wall stile out of the wood into and straight across a field to a wall stile at the top side of trees. Rise uphill to a wall stile and after holly bushes, before a rowan, zigzag left and right downhill onto a distinct path to a three-pillar stone stile in the corner. Turn right and follow the wall (R) for 40 metres. Veer left downhill through mixed trees of Rough Hey Wood. Notice the fantastically contorted trunks of two beech trees close to the left side of the path, shortly after entering the wood.

7. You emerge from the wood onto an old cobble sett trackway. Turn left steeply downhill between walls to the bridge at the bottom – take care: the cobbles can be slippery in any weather or season! Turn right before the bridge, noting a dismantled railway in the cutting (L). At the wall and fence, turn right uphill on a cobbled path. After 100 metres go left through a wall gap with a stone pillar. Go across a field and over stone slabs to a wall stile and back into woodland. Exit through a wall gap with a metal pillar and walk alongside the top of a wall (L) and a fence (R) beside trees. Eventually go up cobbles and steps to turn left onto a cobbled way. Cross a bridge above a culverted stream and continue onto a tarmac road, leading past cottages (L). Notice the horse trough set in the wall (R) just past Upper Wood Nook.

8. Continue onto Long Lane down between walls, with an open view of Sowerby Bridge across the valley. At the road fork, go left downhill, round a right-hand bend and up a tarmac road. At the road junction go right uphill for 40 metres and turn right up a tarmac road on the Link Path to Calderdale Way. Where the tarmac bends left, continue straight ahead up a steep hill on a cobbled path with a stream (L) and wall (R). Go past pillars, concrete (L) and metal (R).

Near the top, in the wall on the right, view Hollin Well, erected by James Wood, AD 1874, with the inscriptions 'Honest Water' and 'Pro Bono Publico'. What is the meaning of this inscription? Whatever the original purpose, the 'well' now gives cattle a good drink! Alternative 'honest water' may be found at the Hobbit public house, 100 metres to the right.

9. Carry on up steps and through an old three-pillar metal stile to turn left onto Hob Lane. Walk on into Harper Royd Lane and immediately past the cottages at Clough Head (R) turn right up a footpath over cobbles and slabs. Go up to a small wooden gate + stone pillar stile (ignoring the gate and stile (R) a few metres before). Follow the path, which at the top turns sharply to the left, climbs three stone steps and passes through a further wooden gate plus three-pillar stile. Veer right up the field. At the top, go through a wooden gate and a wall, and down stone steps onto a lane.

On the next stretch you get a fine view across the valley.

10. Turn right. After 35 metres, go up stone steps left and through a metal gate. Go straight over the field to a telegraph pole, with a small metal gate (L) and alongside the top of a wall (L). Go past two sets of three-stone pillars. Squeeze through stone pillars next to a lower metal

gate (L) and walk alongside a wall (R). Go up to a small metal gate. Note the wall (R) on top of a wooden beam over a water trough, and the row of stones standing vertically on end (L). At the top of the field (L), go through the left-hand of the two small metal gates. Veer right across the field to a fence stile into the car park of The Blue Ball Inn.

Up to your right is Fallingworth Hall, dated 1642, but with MTB 1616 over the porch. To the left is Lower Old Hall, with 1634 GET over its pillared porch.

11. From the car park cross the road straight over onto a track between walls for 80 metres. Go left through a wooden stile, with metal gate (R). Walk diagonally over cobbles down the field to a fence + wall stile. Continue down the field to a fence stile, then down stone steps to a road. Turning right you can either go left down a cobbled road, signposted to Greenhead, and opposite a drive (L) veer up right on a path back onto the road, or follow the road round left.

The Wainhouse Tower above the 'Halifax' building

There is a fine view of the railway viaduct, and of the Wainhouse Tower — what was its original purpose?

12. Bear right and past Pickwood House Farm (L) with butterflies on its wall.

Just past Pickwood Scar Cottages (R) bear left off the road down between walls. Cross a wooden bridge and follow slabs on to go through a wooden gate. Pass a house (L) and, at a Y-junction, take the right-hand fork steadily uphill through the wood. Near the top, in sight of a pylon, turn left over a wall stile back into the wood, signposted North Dean Woods.

The next section is bordered on the left by steep (quarried) cliffs. Just as you emerge from the wood, go to a 'viewpoint' rock (L). There you get a panoramic view of the river, tower, railway viaduct, canal basin, and of the sewage works!

13. Follow the fence (R) as it winds round, then zigzag left and right over a tumbledown wall. At a junction go straight on and eventually go past two sets of wall ends, 50 metres apart. Go straight past 3 metal pillars with stone steps (L), and on past a stone pillar and alongside a wall (R). After the viewpoint, return to the path and veer right on a narrow path between walls which, after two stone pillars, widens out. Veer left at a fork down a lane.

14. Turn acutely right at Bank Top. In 30 metres turn left through a wall and go down stone steps, then wooden steps dropping down under trees. Finally go down stone steps to turn left onto a track. Just before an old metal post (R) pass between stone gate pillars. Immediately turn right down stone steps onto cobble setts (signposted 'Clay House'). Bend left and zigzag left and right down wooden steps. Over to your right is a large pond. Turn left and follow a gravel path above a yard and small industrial buildings. Bend right down the slope, over a wall stile and onto a lane.

Opposite is Clay House (R) – there have been various houses on the site since 13th century and the present house is a fine 17th century building.

Walk through the gardens to the south side of the house. On the far side of a football pitch, a bridge takes you back into the car park.

23: Ogden

The Wind-Farm Walk

Distance: 8.8 km (5½ miles)

Time: 3 hours

Map: OS Outdoor Leisure 21 (1:25 000), Landranger 104 (1:50 000)

Parking: in the public car park at Ogden Reservoir in Ogden Lane, off A629 at The Whole Hog, between Halifax and Denholme, grid reference: 067309

Terrain: farm track and path, field and open moorland, short stretches of road and woodland – undulating with one moderately steep ascent and descent

Refreshments: at The Whole Hog, Ogden Lane, and other hostelries on A629; The Withens, Ovenden Moor

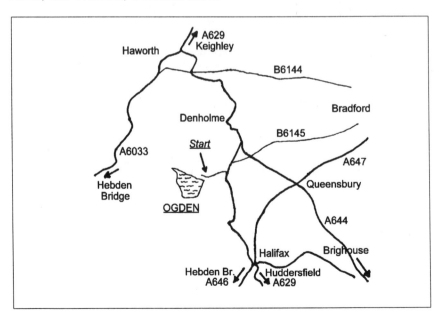

THIS walk is moderately strenuous through a variety of countryside. Starting and finishing at Ogden Reservoir it skirts a golf course, climbs up high to give extensive views on either side of Ovenden Moor including the wind-farm, and returns you down a delightful miniature gorge and through woodland.

Head south down out of the car park on the bridleway to Withens across the dam wall. Go through a metal gate on the far side, then turn left on a footpath. Go straight on, before bending right on a level path round the hillside. Join a broad track downhill to a stone wall (R). The path is not very clear here, but bear down left of a green to a stone hut beside the first tee.

1. In the interests of safety, bear left down a track and before the bridge turn right alongside the stream (L). BEWARE! you are walking along-side the practice ground (R). Continue until you turn left over a concrete bridge, noting the two old clapper bridges beyond. Wind your way round through metal gates past Brook House Farm (R). Turn left up a lane past a stone water trough (L). Immediately on your right go through a wall gap. Keep to the right side of the field going down between fences and over a fence stile. Zigzag right and left to a well-worn wall stile (L). Turn right onto a gravel lane and over a bridge. Walk up into Stod Fold. Go straight on up through a metal gate and up alongside a wall (L) and over slabs to a fence stile. Continue to a stone slab stile. Walk up the field over slabs, left of a tumbledown wall, to a small wooden gate. Turn left for 40 metres and turn sharp right.

Uphill you walk on an old trackway, paved and with grooves on the right-hand track. Further on, to the right of quarry workings is a 'Gap' – why might this be so aptly named?

2. Go over stones and uphill by a stone pillar with slot holes. Going left of a wall and tree, climb up Hunter Hill bending left, with a row of trees (L). Go up through small stone pillars and between walls. Bend to the right of a wall on a trackway. Wind your way through quarry workings. At the very top you come to a small wooden gate. From hereon is a good view across to Stoodley Pike.

3. Turn left and cross the road, then turn acutely right onto a grassy track between walls. Go through stone gateposts and on to a ladder stile and past Planetrees Cottage (L). Continue along the lane and past Spring Mill (R). Bend left and after the cottages turn left for 100 metres. Then turn acutely right and past a ladder stile and Spring Terrace (R). Go

At the head of Ogden Clough

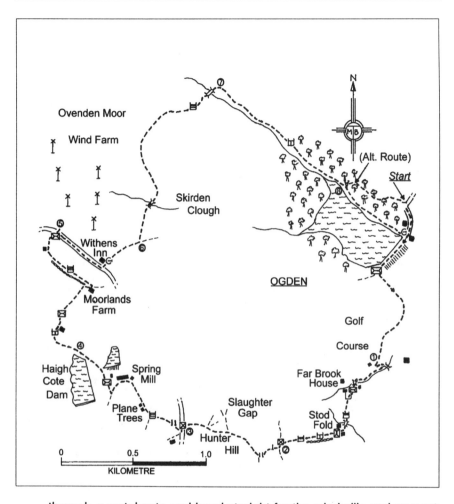

through a metal gate and head straight for the windmills and up past Halifax Water Ski Club at Haigh Cote Dam.

4. Continue on the track and bend right to a fence stile beside the deserted Haigh Cote Farm. Walk on between walls to a metal (once wooden) pole gate. Go right and left round Moorlands Farm: its old barn has a splendid arched doorway with dressed stone and keystones. Turn immediately left beside a wall (L) to a ladder stile over a wall. Go straight on for 200 metres and bear right onto a lane past Withens Head Farm (L) with the inscription TIK 1817. Walk on up and through the metal gate to the road.

Opposite is Ovenden Moor Wind-Farm, located at 430 m (1411 ft) in
an ideal spot on a smooth hilltop with unobstructed exposure to
wind. The average wind speed is 30.76 km per hour, which through
the 23 turbines can generate power for 7500 houses.

5. Turn right down the road - note the pavings with wheel grooves. Go
    down to The Withens Inn, which has a walk-round farm. Turn left across
    the farm and through a wooden kissing gate.

6. In 200 metres turn left onto Ovenden Moor past a fence stile and along a
    track, in parts over slabs. Go over a concrete bridge with iron railings.
    You get a glimpse of Ogden Water (R). Follow the track round to a lad-
    der stile. Go over wooden slats and down a stony path, then steeply
    down stone steps to a bridge with iron railings over a stream.

7. Turn right, following the public footpath sign, to go down into a delightful
    miniature gorge with the stream tumbling down (R). You eventually
    come to a fence stile with a sliding mechanism, and then down over
    slabs to enter Ogden Woodland. Wind your way down through the
    wood, up and down steps. As the track bends up left, take the path down
    right towards the waterside.

8. You come out of the wood on the side of the reservoir, where you have a
    choice of routes: a) continue straight on and pass a feeding area for
    ducks and moorhen, and go through a wooden kissing gate out onto the
    road, where there are toilets, and turn left back up to the car park; or, b)
    follow the path until in 200 metres, on your left go through a stile with a
    sliding mechanism back into the wood, and follow the path diagonally
    right uphill over several streamlets to the car park – note the tree trunks
    carved in the shape of, for example, a ladybird, toadstools and a fox.

24: Norcliffe

The Ancient Monument – Holloway (Magna Via)

Distance: 8 km (5 miles)

Time: 2½ hours

Map: OS Explorer 288 (1:25 000), Landranger 104 (1:50 000),

Parking: in Hipperholme take the A58 west for some 200 metres and turn left into Halifax Old Road, down Tan House Hill towards Shibden Hall. In a further 200 metres turn left over an old railway bridge, and then take the first on the right steeply down Badger Lane. Norcliffe Lane is ahead in the dip of the lane. Park at any convenient spot, grid reference: 118253

Terrain: meadow and field, farm track, path and short stretches of road – the walk is level at the beginning over generally easy ground, followed by a steep uphill section and a moderate descent

Refreshments: The Travellers on Halifax Old Road; Malt Shovel in Southowram

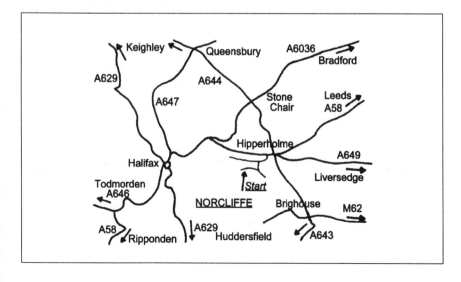

THIS walk is easy in the early stages taking you along a valley bottom. The middle section takes you steeply uphill. At the top, close to Southowram you gain good views over the valley. On the way back via Sunny Bank you descend on a notable former trackway.

Starting in the dip of the road, facing south, walk straight ahead on a lane, initially concreted, then flagged and cobbled, alongside a stream (L). As the lane bends right at metal railings, veer left onto a

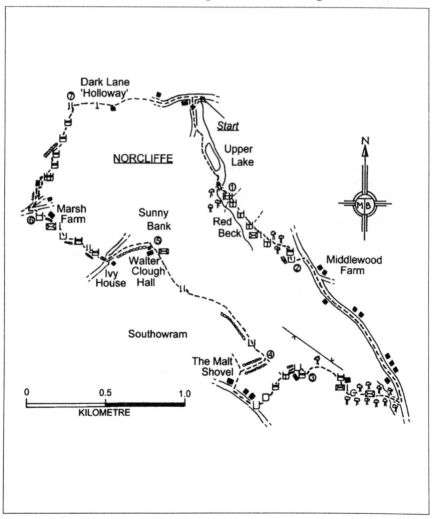

track and through zigzag fences. Walk past the right-hand side of a
large overgrown pond, complete with island and rhododendrons.
This area, known as Sunnyvale, was a popular location for days out
in the 1930s and 1940s, and it included a café and a maze. At the far
end, where slabs are stacked, turn right at a signpost directing you to
Walter Clough Lane. Bend left, down stone steps and over a wooden
bridge, and then wind through under trees beside the stream (R).

1. Go through a zigzag fence and over the lane to a fence stile, signposted
    Brookfoot, keeping to the left of the stream. Go on to a fence stile and
    continue over stone slabs and a field. After another fence stile, a stream
    disappears into the ground (L) and steps come down from the left. The
    ground ahead is boggy. Go on until you go through stone pillars with
    postholes, with a wooden gate (R). Go across the meadow to a fence
    stile. Bear upwards left through trees and on to a stile of large vertical
    stone slabs. Go on to a tarmac lane past stables (R) and through a gap
    between a wooden gate (L) and a wall (R) with metal pillars.

2. Going up left, turn right onto the road past Red Belk House (R) and fur-
    ther on Middlewood Farm (L). Carry on through houses until just before
    factories, make an acute right turn down a farm track through trees.
    Keep going with the bends, through a metal gate and between
    fence/railings. Go over a stream and up a paved path (old trackway?)
    and through a metal kissing gate. Emerge from trees/bushes and go
    through a gap between a metal gate (L) and stone pillar. Veer right and
    to a wall stile, with wooden farm gate (R). Bending slightly left round
    walls, veer left uphill to go left of a pylon. As you go up more steeply left
    of a lone tree, enjoy the view.

3. Cross a wall stile in front of a white house and turn right onto a terrace
    and then between high stone walls. Go left through a wall gap and up
    stone steps between narrowing walls. Go up a grassy track ahead to a
    fence stile in the top left-hand corner. Continue straight on up the field,
    with a quarry (L). Cross a slab wall stile and go right of and alongside a
    garden wall (L) to a small wooden gate. Go up the ginnel between stone
    walls to a gap in the wall at the road. Turn right for 60 metres to The Malt
    Shovel. Turn right into Cross Platts down between walls. When you
    reach carved stone posts and a pointed metal pillar (L), turn right down
    a track between walls.

    Note the good example of grooves cut into the stone slabs by
    wheels.

4. Bend left and, where the track starts to go downhill, go left into the field;

you may choose to do this by climbing over the metal gate or the low
wall to its right. Follow the wall (L) on to go past stone pillars and a stile
(L) under power lines, through gateposts and veer right to a lone tree
and round to a farm. Squeeze between a wall (L) and a metal gate (R).
Go through the farm buildings of Walter Clough Hall to a junction.

5.   Turn left up the lane past a wall (L). At the end turn left on the road for 10
     metres, then turn right up steps (on a Link Path) and past a stone pillar
     with markings. Go up the field over slabs to a slab pillar stile in the
     right-hand corner - note the vertical slab wall (L). Go left up a wall (L)
     and through a stone pillar stile. Walk diagonally right to a stone pillar
     and slab stile. Go left up the wall (L) to a wall gap with a stone pillar. Veer
     right over the field to a stone pillar stile, beside an ornamental metal
     gate (L). Go over stone slabs, with a large house over the wall (R), to a
     fence stile onto a tarmac drive. Turn left at Marsh Farm.

6.   Go up to the junction and turn sharp right downhill (Marsh Lane). After
     20 metres, turn left on a narrow path between fences. At a broad track
     turn right and immediately left alongside houses. At the last house, fol-
     low a path left between walls. Then at once turn right and zigzag
     through a wall stile to go diagonally right over stone slabs and on over
     the field. You come to a stone slab stile with steps. Turn left along a ter-
     race to squeeze through another slab stile with a huge wall (L). Carry on
     between walls to a stone pillar stile. At one point cross over a small wall
     stile to go between walls and under pylons. Go past pillars out onto a
     track.

     On this stretch you gain a good view down over Hipperholme.

7.   You now turn right down Dark Lane, an ancient monument known as
     Holloway, 'hollowed out' by centuries of traffic. This Lane is the
     Wakefield Gate to the Magna Via, which was until the 18th century the
     only road going eastwards out of Halifax. You walk down over a mixture
     of cobbles and slabs, but BEWARE—they may be slippery, as noted by
     Daniel Defoe in 1724! Note the commemorative plaque (L) at the foot of
     the Lane - what is historically wrong on this plaque?

     Continue on and bear left down the road onto Norcliffe Lane and to
     wherever you have parked your car.

25: Norwood Green

The Figure-of-Eight Walk

Distance: 11.2 km (7 miles), or 5.6 km (3½ miles) if split into two walks

Time: 3½ hours (or 1½ and 2 hours, if walked separately)

Map: OS Explorer 288 (1:25 000), Landranger 104 (1:50 000)

Parking: in the vicinity of The Olde Beare, Village Street, Norwood Green

Terrain: meadow and field, farm track, path and short stretches of road — undulating on the first section; the second starts with a steepish descent followed by a moderate incline up to the ridge at Coley; after two woodland valleys it is a gentle stroll back into Norwood Green

Refreshments: at The Olde Beare, Norwood Green

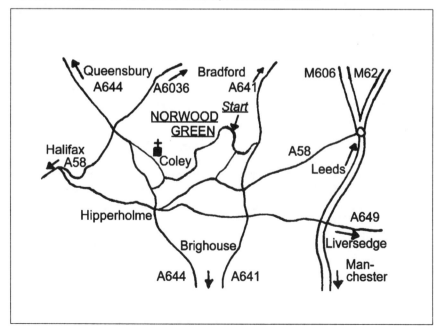

THIS walk is relatively easy starting and finishing in the attractive village of Norwood Green. On the first section it takes you under and over the railway and through two very pleasant stretches of woodland. On the second section it drops you steeply into a valley before taking you up in a long arc to Coley Church. From here you pass through two delightful woodland stretches, the second of which can take you past a most picturesque, and quite unexpected, waterfall.

First Section: Map A – Starting with The Olde Beare to your left, cross and walk down Village Street until just beyond Thorn Garth (R) turn right on a public footpath signposted on a small stone set in the ground. Go down the backs of cottages (L) and past a farm gate, across a field and through a hawthorn hedge to two fence stiles at right angles. Turn left along the top side of the wood to a zigzag fence stile with a stone pillar.

View the churches away to your right: St John's, Coley (far right), the (former) United Reformed Church, and St Matthew's, Lightcliffe; and Castle Hill Tower, slightly left, just visible in the distance.

1.   Crossing the field bend round left to a fence stile. Go on over slabs to a small fence gate between a wall (L) and a metal gate (R). Turn right into Rookes Lane, passing Rookes Hall (R) and Lower Rookes Farm (L). Take care in crossing A58. Go left for 20 metres, then right onto tarmac lane and eventually between walls and under the railway. Follow the lane round to the right between overgrown walls, past a metal gate and on downhill under trees. Wind round to a concrete bridge with metal railings over a stream and up slabs fairly steeply to pass Bottom Hall Farm and Cottage (R).

2.   Over the top opposite Till Carr Cottage (dated 1634), squeeze left through stone pillars and follow the wall (L) across the field. Go through a wall gap with a metal pillar and straight on for 20 metres to go left through a wooden kissing gate. Walk straight on but then bend right on a terrace trackway to the bottom and go over metal railings at a bridge with substantial stone parapets.

3.   At a corner of an estate wall (R) turn left across a stream on a large slab bridge with metal railings. Walk up to a fence stile, carrying straight on left of a hedge and pole, then veer right between hawthorn and bramble bushes. Follow the hawthorn (R) to go through a wall gap with pillar. Carry on across the field up to a fence gate. Again cross A58 and go through a fence gate onto the Calderdale Way. Veer left up the field,

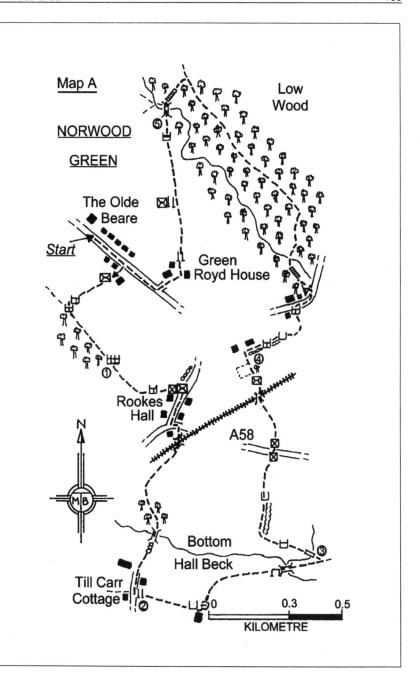

Map A

NORWOOD

GREEN

Low Wood

The Olde
● Beare

Start

Green
Royd House

Rookes
Hall

A58

N

M B

Bottom
Hall Beck

Till Carr
Cottage

0   0.3   0.5
KILOMETRE

eventually left of hawthorn and up past posts and over the railway. At the other side of the bridge go past a wooden farm gate. Go up, round and through trees to pass a cricket pitch (L).

You can see over to the village of Wyke (R). Up on your left is a 'period' mansion with certain interesting features. In 0.5 km or so, you enter a delightful woodland. What is the local name of this woodland?

4. Before a white farm gate turn right to go onto a grassy track between walls to a fence stile. Keep down the line of the hedge (R), to squeeze through a wall and down a step. Go right and left round a shed to bend left to a fence stile. Turn right onto the road, bending round left. Almost in the dip, cross a V-shaped fence stile (L) into Low Wood. Go down wooden steps and past a seat under a spreading beech tree. Continue on a high embankment over a stream and up to a signpost where you turn left. Carry on a clearly made path, over wooden planks and past another seat (R). Winding round and past yet another seat (L) you come to a junction of tracks. Turn left and down stone steps with a wall (R) and bend left to cross a bridge.

5. Go straight on to cross a wall stile and on up through hawthorn bushes over a red brick core. Go round a wooden pillar stile beside a metal farm gate (R). Over the crest of the hill you come to another wooden pillar stile in the corner of a garden. Go on the left side of a farmhouse (Green Royd) (R) and pass various buildings (L). Veer right on a stony drive to turn right back onto Village Street and up to wherever you have parked your car.

    Second Section: if you wish to carry on, or even start at this point, use **Map B**.

    Walk north east along Village Street, round a left bend and on until it changes into Norwood Green Hill. Bend down left past Chatsworth House (L) — yes, really! In 20 metres turn right into Queens Road, at the bottom of which you fork right and go down a ginnel, through stone pillars and down steps to Coley Beck Cottage (R). Go left down the lane to turn right into Shutts Lane – BEWARE slippery flagstones! – and over the bridge. Go up past Coley Mill Cottage (L) with a cock weather vane on the garage.

1. As the road bends right, turn sharp left round the tree through a hidden squeeze wall stile and between hedges. Continue to a stone slab stile in a fence. Turn right and go up the field past a line of trees (R). After the fifth tree (marked with a yellow rectangle), follow the path on a leftward bend towards a small metal gate by the corner of the wall. Follow the

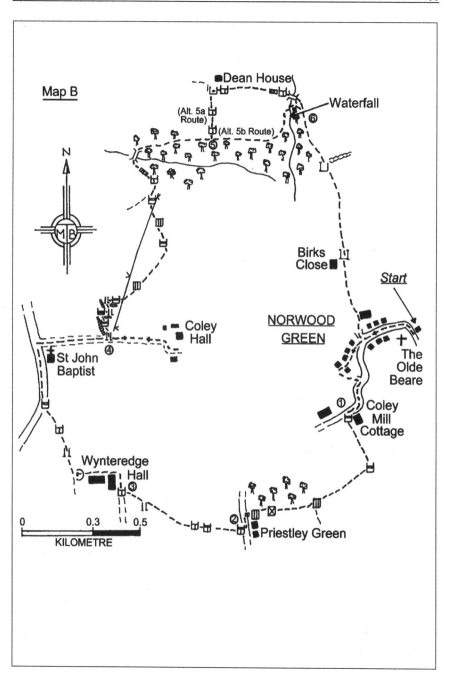

Map B

Dean House

(Alt. 5a Route)
(Alt. 5b Route)

Waterfall
⑥

N

Birks
Close

Start

NORWOOD
GREEN

The
Olde
Beare

Coley
Hall

St John
Baptist
④

①

Coley
Mill
Cottage

Wynteredge
Hall
③

②

Priestley Green

0   0.3   0.5
KILOMETRE

wall (R), well-built but now somewhat buckled by trees, with a large 'period' residence over it. Also look left to see the old windows in the original part of the house (L). At the top of the field go through a wooden gate and over a side garden to a tall metal mesh gate. Go up steps, turn left into Shutts Lane (Priestley Green) for 50 metres.

2. Just before the junction with Syke Lane, turn right up and over a slab wall + fence stile through the hedge. Follow the line of trees up the field to a wall + fence stile, then a fence stile on the other side of a ditch. Continue up the field to and through 2 stone pillars with postholes and upright stone slabs (R). Crossing another field diagonally, go over the fence stile to turn right into the lane.

To your left is a superb old house (Wynteredge Hall). The barn has dove ledges and holes over the main door, and is topped by a fine weather vane. Note the stained glass windows on the track past the rear of the hall. Further on, enjoy the view across the valley to Halifax. Before the church, in the front courtyard of Poplars see the old stone trough set in the wall.

3. Walk on to turn left round the first building and up a broad track past the rear of the hall. At the end go through a metal kissing gate and turn right

Wynteredge Hall

with the wall, built round trees! Go on through stone pillars. Cross the fence stile and then a wall stile, and continue straight ahead on the road past Chapel House Farm (R). Immediately past St John the Baptist Church turn right down a public bridleway between stone pillars and down the broad track. Before you go under the pylon wires, turn left through a stone pillar stile.

A suggested detour, before going through the stile, is to go on down the bridleway for a further 300 metres and round the dog-leg, to view Coley Hall — the most impressive house in the area. Retrace your steps.

4. Once through the stile, with a metal gate (R), the right of way is intriguingly tortuous! Follow the wall (L) and cross two wall stiles. Turn right at a wall (R) following it round to a stone pillar stile. Again follow the wall (L) through a stone pillar stile. Turn right following the wall (R) to a slab stile. Veer left across the field, keeping to the right of a pylon down to a wall stile over a stream and to a metal mesh gate. Follow the path that runs parallel to the stream (R), bending left towards a pylon and through a wall stile beside a holly bush (R). Go on to a metal mesh gate and a wall stile with a metal pillar. Go under the pylon, round right with the wall past a stone pillar with postholes to a fence stile and into a wood. Follow the main path down to the left and past seats (R and L); after the second go right down and over stepping stones; turn right by a third seat and over a wooden bridge. Go uphill and at the top of the slope you have a choice of paths:

5a. Technically, the path bends left through holly bushes to a fence stile out of the wood and on to a fence stile and alongside a fence/wall (R). Before the end of the wall with a gate ahead, turn right up through a wall gap and over a fence stile to follow the wall (L). Then go over a collapsed wall with wall (R) and straight ahead down the field and stone steps. You come to a fence stile and wooden bridge across a stream. Turn right and veer left of the overgrown ruins of a small building — you can hear a waterfall down to your right. You may choose to go and view it, but do take care.

5b. Alternatively, take the right fork past the left edge of the wood. The path bends left. Shortly and unexpectedly a gorgeous waterfall comes into view, with its rock face covered in moss and lichen, BUT do take care as the banks are somewhat undercut! Once you have had your fill, pass on to cross the stream and go left and then turn right sharply uphill round the overgrown ruins of an old building.

Once you have emerged from the wood and onto high ground, you get brief glimpses of Castle Hill and Emley Mast, both south of Huddersfield.

6. At the top of the slope, bear right and shortly by a wall (L) veer left up and out of the wood, aiming left of a pylon. Go through a gap in the wall with a stone pillar. Continue on the Calderdale Way alongside a wall to squeeze between a stone pillar and fence. Go between a fence/hedge (L) and hedge (R). Go through a wall gap with pillars and onto a flagged and dirt track between walls — note the grooves in the slabs on the second section. You emerge past Lower Ox Heys Farm with its horse weather vane on the garage (L). Also note the elaborate stone pillar stile at the entrance to the lane (R). At the road turn left up Norwood Green Hill and return to wherever you have parked your car.

26: Shibden

A Hall and a Tunnel

Distance: 9.6 km (6 miles)

Time: 3 hours

Map: OS Explorer 288 (1:25 000), Landranger 104 (1:50 000)

Parking: in the bottom car park of Shibden Hall Park, off A58 between Halifax and Hipperholme

Terrain: meadow and field, farm track, path and stretches of road – the walk is undulating with considerable stretches of level ground combined with some short steepish uphill pulls and one moderate downhill stretch

Refreshments: at the Shibden Hall tea room, the Stump Cross Inn on A58, and The Shibden Mill Inn (Restaurant) after 2 km

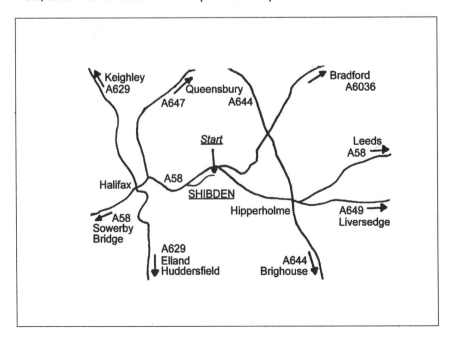

A gate on the Shibden Walk

THIS most pleasant walk starts and finishes in the grounds of the 15th century Shibden Hall, once occupied by the Otes family – well worth a visit together with its Folk Museum. The route takes you up the picturesque Shibden Dale almost to its head. Once at the top you see many former quarry workings. You return along parts of the Calderdale Way, skirting Northowram before descending through more pleasant woodland. Once back into Shibden Shout, there are other attractions, including a miniature railway, boating pool and pitch/putt course.

Go out of the car park in a north-westerly direction through a corner exit into a road (Red Beck Road). At the junction, go up steps across the road. Immediately turn left going steeply up alongside an ivy covered wall (R) and up steps to the main road (A58). Take care in crossing this. Go through a wall gap, signposted to Shibden Fold, and left down a cobbled path with a metal handrail (R). At the bottom turn right round a lamppost and stone pillar in mid-path onto a grassy path. Look across to your right to see the house with its mullion-type windows.

1. At the junction with the tarmac go straight on past the farm buildings (R) and Rose Cottage (L). Go up the track between walls to a wooden gate between wooden pillars, next to a larger barred gate. Walk on over slabs to a vertical zigzag slab stile. Continue across the field on slabs to a wall stile beside a wooden pillar. As you cross the next field note the stone slab with the double headed arrow between W and D. Note the stream tumbling out of the wall (L) as you go up the stone steps to a wooden gate through a wall.

2. Carry on over slabs to come out onto the farm track. Follow this through gateposts and onto a double slabbed pavement between walls. Go down right and left – stone trough in the wall (L) – and over a bridge into Horley Green Lane. Walk through the car park of Shibden Mill Inn (R). Carry on up and left into the road following it round left and right – ignoring Whiskers Lane (R) – on into Simm Carr Lane. Carry on up the road alongside the stream (L) and right round up past Lower Lime House (L). Continue steeply up the track ahead. At the fork bear left, always keeping to the main track and ignoring gateposts (R) and (L).

As you continue upwards, the upper end of Shibden Dale is down to your left.

3. Bending right you come alongside a high wall, and almost immediately turn right up through a flagged tunnel – why such a remarkable feature?

Go up stone steps and between the wall and large vertical slab stones to a stile topped by a metal bar. Continue up the field to go through a wall gap made of a slab (L) and stone pillar (R). Finally go over a fence stile to turn right into Green Lane.

Just above Upper Northroyd Farm (R) are imposing carved gateposts with postholes. Down the first lane (L) is a magnificent house dated 1692.

4. Continue down the road until you turn left into Paddock Road. As it bends right, go up left for 20 metres to squeeze right between a fence (L) and wall (R). Follow the line of the wall up to a wall stile. At cross-tracks go straight on a path between holly bushes. At the end veer left up a former trackway between walls, the left one being particularly well-built. Bend round left and at cross-paths turn right down past Newton Hill (R). Take the right fork and cross the road to go through a wall gap onto the Calderdale Way.

5. Going over slabs, pass a stone trough and go over a wall stile, turning right down over slabs. At the farm gate (R) turn left onto the farm track and on through gateposts. Carry on past a wall corner (L) to squeeze through a wall gap. Notice the vertical slab wall (L) and the slabs (R) propping up the trees. Go through a zigzag vertical slab stile to a stone carved pillar stile. Continue to exit through metal pillars onto Score Hill. Turn right.

6. Crossing the road, just before the 'slippery road ahead' sign, turn left alongside a hedge (R) to squeeze past a white farm gate (L). Go beside a wall (R) to a wall stile in the corner, alongside the wall to another wall stile, and on to a wall gap beside a pylon (R). Keep right of the hawthorn bushes to come out onto the road by the corner of a wall of large shale blocks. Cross the road and turn right for 20 metres. Go left over the wall winding round close to the works site (L). Bend round left and go down and right between low walls, to emerge through a small metal mesh gate; this gate is easily missed – an alternative path simply goes over the wall and brings you to the same place. Cross the field to go between wooden pillars and down stone steps to another small metal mesh gate.

7. Turn acutely right and across the field to the corner of a wall (R). Go straight across the field over slabs to a zigzag stone stile in the corner with stone steps down and on between walls and cottages on to a lane, which bends left and round past Westercroft House. On a left-hand wall is a metal bracket with a horse and rider jumping a fence. At the road turn right for 80 metres, then left past the side of a cricket field. Over a

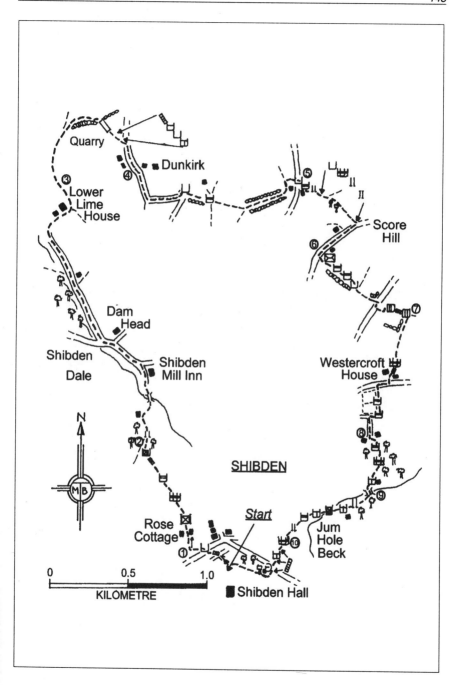

wall stile go past another! cricket field. Going over a wall stile turn right for 50 metres and then left down a tarmac lane.

8.   At the bend, veer leftish onto the grass alongside a hedge (R) and to the path into the corner. The path bends right downhill through the trees, bending left to a side-on wall stile and down between wire fences to a side-on zigzag wall stile. Go left through this until, turning right, you follow a hawthorn hedge (R) for 50 metres. Go down to the bottom of the hillside to a fence stile in front of stone cottages. Turn right into the lane and then left down a concrete track. Note the waterfall (R). Go on down past a horse parade ring (L) and over a bridge.

9.   Immediately bend right onto a path. Cross two slabs over the stream and cross the bottom of the field keeping to the right of a telegraph pole. When you reach a stream, go through a stone pillar stile on the right of a fence stile; over another stream and up over slabs to a small fence gate in a wall; over yet another stream to a fence stile in a hedge. Veer right uphill to a vertical stone slab over a wall. Walk over slabs and squeeze between wooden pillars beside a wall (R). There is a cock weather vane on a barn (L). You then come to a zigzag wall stile.

10.   Follow the line of the fence, then hedge (L), to go down stone steps, over a fence stile and down more steps. Cross the road, turning right for 10 metres. Go left and through a metal kissing gate down a ginnel between walls with a black and white timbered house (R). Walk down several flights of stone steps, bending right into Shibden Park. You can now choose your own route back to the car park.

Also of Interest:

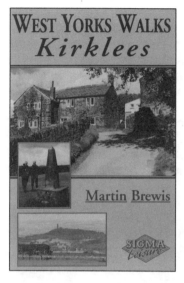

Companion volume!

WEST YORKS WALKS: KIRKLEES

Martin Brewis

Pick up this guidebook, pull on your boots and get away from it all in 'Last of the Summer Wine' country! These 26 walks are all circular, range from 3 to 7 miles, and will help you discover the diverse beauty of the area. From walks centred on the secluded towns and villages in the Holme, Colne and Spen valleys to spectacular panoramic views from high ridges, there's a walk to grab everyone's imagination.
£6.95

BEST TEA SHOP WALKS IN WEST YORKSHIRE

Norman & June Buckley

A further volume in the now well-established tea shop walks series, covering part of the South Pennine area of first-class walking country, linked with selected tea shops in the towns and villages.

Easy-going walks are complemented by enjoyable and unusual tea shops en route. Full descriptions are given of the tempting delicacies that await the hungry walker.
£6.95

TOWNS AND VILLAGES OF BRITAIN: WEST YORKSHIRE

John Spencer

This title is the essential guide to West Yorkshire as seen through the colourful history of its towns and villages. Although written in a lively, readable style, it's comprehensive and presented in an easy-to-use reference book format. Over 300 entries cover all the main settlements of the county, highlighting the key buildings, landscape and famous personalities of the area, together with associated folklore and legends.
£6.95

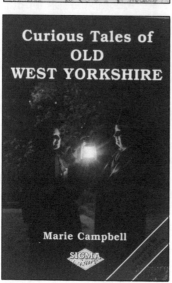

CURIOUS TALES OF OLD WEST YORKSHIRE

Marie Campbell

"A fascinating collection of odd tales of occult doings, curious clergymen, eccentrics and the allsorts of society's fringes." NORTHERN EARTH 1999
"In this fascinating, entertaining, bustling...package of oddities, Marie Campbell ranges far and wide." BRADFORD TELEGRAPH & ARGUS
£7.95

All of our books are available through booksellers. In case of difficulty, or for a free catalogue, please contact:
SIGMA LEISURE, 1 SOUTH OAK LANE, WILMSLOW, CHESHIRE SK9 6AR.
Phone: 01625-531035
Fax: 01625-536800.
E-mail: info@sigmapress.co.uk
Web site: http//www.sigmapress.co.uk
MASTERCARD and VISA orders welcome.